ALWAYS FORWARD!

DISCOVER THE 7 SECRETS OF SALES SUCCESS

William S. Wooditch

INDIE BOOKS
INTERNATIONAL

ISBN: 1-941870-45-7
ISBN-13: 978-1-941870-45-7
LOC: 2015956150

Designed by Joni McPherson, mcphersongraphics.com

INDIE BOOKS INTERNATIONAL, LLC
2424 VISTA WAY, SUITE 316
OCEANSIDE, CA 92054
www.indiebooksintl.com

DEDICATION

To my sister Mary, the author in the family—she looked into the face of fear and found the courage to pursue her dreams. Without her encouragement, support, and guidance, I would still be stuck in the intent phase of writing.

CONTENTS

A LETTER TO THE READER

This book will show you the way to win. It will reveal the way through seven secrets that will provide you with an edge in your business and personal pursuits. If you are ready to make the commitment required to move forward in sales, this book will serve as both your essential toolkit and indispensable guide.

I am not a consultant. I am an active participant in the game of business. Each secret has been battle-tested in over twenty-four years of in-the-trenches face-to-face engagement. The hard-won lessons in the book are designed to alleviate the pain and shorten the distance between where you are now and where you are determined to go in the future. These secrets can create the foundation for an exciting and rewarding life if you are willing to face your fear and become compelled to move forward.

Fear distracts our attention and derails the pursuit of progress. At stake is the difference between a life and an existence. I am reminded of a story about a magnificent lion regaled in John Eldredge's *Wild at Heart*. This lion roamed free on the plains of Africa—king of all he surveyed. He was taken into captivity and placed in a zoo where thousands of people looked on his forced sequestration with awe and reverence, perhaps some with a profound sadness. After a short period of time, the lion refused to eat. The fire from his spirit seemed to evaporate daily. He became lethargic. The lion gave up on life, the ever-dimming light of his eyes peering through the bars of captivity.

You are neither more nor less than you choose to reveal. Choose to reveal the authentic you, the one not subject to the limits of fear or governed by the insecurity of ego. Find alignment with your true nature. When you find and live in the spirit of this alignment, your purpose will ensue; you will feel your pulse and find your passion.

Live a life that absorbs the energy of fear as fuel and moves, *Always Forward!*

William S. Wooditch

PART I

FACING FEAR

"Fear is the tool of a man-made devil. Self-confident faith in one's self is both the man-made weapon which defeats this devil and the man-made tool which builds a triumphant life. And it is more than that. It is a link to the irresistible forces of the universe which stand behind a man who does not believe in failure and defeat as being anything but temporary experiences."

— **Napoleon Hill**

MAKE THE COMMITMENT TO FACE DOWN FEAR

T housands of soldiers in scarlet tunics and gold helmets, on foot and on horseback, were amassed on the banks of the Rubicon River at the edge of Rome. In the year 49 BC, Julius Caesar, then governor of Gaul (modern day France), had been ordered by the Roman Senate to disband his army or be declared an enemy of the state. His ambitions for power were driving him forward, but his fear of the consequences of civil war gave him pause. He had halted at the edge of the river to ruminate on the importance of this decision. The river was the dividing line between Rome and the Italian frontier, and Caesar knew it was forbidden by the Roman Senate for any standing army to enter into Rome. That stream was the line of demarcation—once that line was crossed there was no going back. It was move forward, conquer, or be destroyed.

The troops knew this rule as well. They were battle-hardened soldiers, caked in the dried blood and mud of conquest, the residual of eight years of sacrifice and struggle. United cause forges loyalty on the anvil of shared hardship. The legions would follow Caesar wherever he would lead. According to ancient historians, Caesar cried out to his troops, "Let us go where the omens of the Gods and the crimes of our enemies summon us! The die is now cast!" With that, Caesar crossed the Rubicon, signaling the start of a civil war that would change Rome from a republic to an empire. Retreat was not an option—the die had been cast.

Caesar moved forward across that stream and into the pages of history. In business, "Crossing the Rubicon" is referenced as the ultimate commitment. It means there's no way back, no retreat, no surrender. When you make that commitment, you don't look for an exit strategy. You may fail, but you must keep moving forward. It's the risk you must take and the minimum level of commitment you must make to create success in your life.

If you are to create a difference in life, you must cross your Rubicon. The Rubicon must be crossed before you apply for a new position, enter a client's office, or walk the job floor. It must be crossed before you walk down the aisle and say, "I do." Congruency of action in all walks of life prevents the fractures that breed discontent and ambiguity. You must cross the Rubicon-you must commit. You have to cross the Rubicon—you have to commit. Life is a spectator sport unless you commit. Choose to be a participant—become engaged and have fun in the process.

Progress is initiated through decisive action; it's the hardest won of victories but the sweetest fruit of conquest. When you live your life in the way of congruence—a way that is centered on values, anchored by character, and expressed as genuine—you are living without fracture, living and thriving through alignment. Your integrity, character, and authenticity can make for the very best of you. When you are congruent from thought to word and word to action, others can be magnetically pulled and influenced by the consistency and vibrancy of your nature.

DIFFERENCE MAKERS

When Caesar stood on the banks of the river, do you think he was immune to fear? I imagine he felt an unsettling fear, but he did not allow it to undermine his resolve. It is easy to become stymied by pervasive thoughts of failure. Difference makers subjugate the feeling of fear by summoning the resolve to move through the inertia of uncertainty and the reluctant lure of resistance. They move through fears, assess and address the risks and take the initiative.

You are the guardian of your own success. Success demands your attention and strength of resolve. You don't cross the threshold to success from the land of wish and hope—you cross from the place of, "If it is to be, it is up to me." Are you willing to pay the toll? Are you willing to make the sacrifice? Do you have what it takes: an insatiable curiosity, a willingness to learn, a determination to apply, a deep need to achieve, and the willpower to follow through on each and every commitment?

There is a soft underbelly that can accompany success. It is comprised of comfort and takes shape from the mindset that success is a destination, not an ongoing quest. Success doesn't have a pause button. We are either moving forward toward a goal or we are becoming more estranged from it. At a minimum, to maintain the status-quo requires the willingness to learn, apply and pay the price of success by pushing through barriers of comfort. Those unwilling to pay the price will become mired in the stalled motivation of mediocrity. Find verve, hone your vision, exert willpower and export your message through purpose-driven execution. Make today's hurdle to greatness tomorrow's bar of expectation!

People who don't succeed often blame bad luck and condition as the reason. When we compare ourselves to others, we are working off of life's curve, an average born of the expectation we assume from the assessment of the behavior we experience from others. Choose instead to be a better version of yourself today than you were yesterday and take the steps to become a better you tomorrow than you are today. Comparing yourself to others is a useless, frustrating no-win game of relative comparison. It creates frustration, anger, disappointment and an external version of self-worth that is ephemeral at best.

"Life is divided into three terms—that which was, which is, and which will be. Let us learn from the past to profit by the present, and from the present to live better in the future."

— William Wordsworth

The ones who make it have a strong need to prove or validate their self-worth—they have a confidence and a strong conviction of purpose that becomes the intangible product people feel and support. They have the willingness to consistently do those things they may not want to do and hold themselves accountable to the habits that separate those who can and do from those who don't and won't. They commit and become pulled by purpose, compelled to do that which they must. They have the willpower to continue to do what it takes with a high degree of effective energy and directed commitment, day in and day out. The winner does not allow events outside of their control to define their self-worth—they know they may fail, but failure doesn't dominate their thoughts; learning how to win does. When they fail, they learn from it. They don't call it failure—they call it a learning experience.

One of your strongest weapons against fear is to become compelled to fulfill your purpose. If the pull from your purpose is stronger than the resistance of fear, you will move forward. The great ones are driven from the pull of purpose—they are compelled to make their purpose a reality. Pursuit from purpose will transcend the uncertainty that creates delay from fear. Make things happen by dispatching the noise and nuisance of fear. Your quality of life will be dictated by the stronger pull—you will either move forward from compelling conviction through fear, or you will lose your nerve and succumb to the resistance.

LIGHTS, CAMERA, LIFE

No matter how intrepid we may be, we have fears, shadows of doubt, and perhaps for some of us, deep seeds of insecurity. We either exist within the limits of our fears or live to the promise of our potential. Some may live lives without happiness, joy, and pleasure, but few of us can escape the grip of fear. We all have our fears—they just vary by degree and severity. Fear can cause our minds to drift, amble, stumble, and then run down the path of worst-case scenarios. Attempting to run from these is to flee from our obligation to understand, accept, and contain the emotion. If we risk certainty and begin to take action, we can steer through our fears instead of allowing them to chase us into the shadows.

We have the choice to become the screenwriters, directors, and protagonists in the movies of our lives. We also have the choice to relinquish the screenwriting duties to someone else, take direction from another, and become an extra in the movie. The choice is ours. With each passing moment, we create the roles we choose in the movies of our lives. We choose the direction, the development, and by doing so, the plot and denouement, or final act. Fear can become the social drama we play out through unchecked thoughts and feelings, or it can be understood, accepted, contained, and navigated to live a life of increase. The experience of moving through one fear can become a guide to moving through all fears. What a great gift! Our present situation and station in life is a product of previous attempts and steps. Were some of those steps risky? Were some of those steps rewarding? The only real sense of certainty we can have in a world fraught with uncertainty will be dictated by our willingness to take decisive steps and do what the gut feels and the head believes to be worthy of pursuit.

Every move provides the chance to change your life just by the nature of movement. Those steps forward change the environment—make yours an environment that is prosperous and profitable. Have some fun along the way—life is to live, not endure.

The only person in the story of your life who can develop the plot and change the outcome is you. If you feel that gnawing sense of uncertainty in your gut and maybe shrug it off and say, "I can't," well then you won't. "I can't do this," "I don't know enough," "It's too hard," "I'm too old," "I'm not experienced enough," "It's too late"—you will be correct in every case; fear wins, game over. I think the fun, the purpose of life is to live it. Get out there and really give the effort. Choose to develop and deploy the mental and physical resources that will make a difference in your life.

Fear told Richard Branson not to start Virgin Airlines; he didn't listen to the voice. Fear told George Washington he wouldn't survive the winter, but he got on that boat at Valley Forge, and we're living today from the courage of his historical move forward.

RESISTANCE CHECKPOINT

Are you ready to make a commitment to yourself? If you already have made a commitment, revisit the commitment as a goal until you achieve it. Commit to accomplishing that goal every day, and you will find or make a way to win some part of the game of life.

SAWDUST AND LACQUER

I crossed my Rubicon when I left home in my late teens. There was no going back unless it was on my proverbial shield. I grew up in Kane, a borough in Western Pennsylvania. What is a borough? Well, Kane's population fluctuates between 3,600 and 4,200, depending upon time of year. The winter fun is reserved for the locals. The summer brings in a few tourists. Located in the middle of a forest, Kane's main source of income is derived from the lumber industry. It is a rustic paradise where one can find isolation among the trees in the forest. I thought I was cool, didn't want to go to school, grew my hair, started smoking cigarettes, and cashed my checks from the woodworking factory at the bar with my friends every other Friday.

Every day, I forced myself up at five o'clock in the morning—somewhere between the fog of deep slumber and a mindless zombie trance. I put on a wool coat and a yellow hat with the moniker "Miles Ahead" inscribed on it and assumed a sleepwalking trudge to the factory. There are few things that can wake a person up like the smell of sawdust and lacquer finish. When the doors opened, these distinctive scents welcomed me onto the floor.

BROWN BAGS

My factory existence consisted of punching a clock when I trudged in, boredom, a lunch break, extended periods of boredom, a lunch break, followed by more boredom, and then I punched that clock again when I dragged my tired butt out. Not only was the work the same every day, but my dietary habits conformed to convenience and affordability. The brown bags I opened each day at lunch contained sandwiches with thin slices of bologna. Perhaps, if it was payday, I splurged and added a slice of cheese.

In my job, I punched three holes in a piece of wood that was about eighteen inches long and one inch thick for eight hours a day. I produced three hundred pieces of acceptable product each day. No deviation—just fit, punch, push, punch, push, punch. I discarded the defective pieces in a pile and continued punching, fitting, and pushing product. I had less defective product than some of my coworkers, and as a reward I was promoted to the paint room. I sprayed veneer over some pre-fab pieces of wood for eight hours a day.

During this mind-numbing, repetitive process, I began to use my imagination to visualize and transcend the rote requirements of the job. Most teenage thoughts are discursive, ranging from sex to food and sleep. In addition to these omnipresent hormonal imperatives, I ran a mental play-by-play of entire football games to keep my brain active. Other times I imagined something outside of the forest, the factory floors, outside of the chain-smoking, long-haired rabble, and the collection of fellow malcontents that sat around the break room.

Every day I woke up and knew what I feared: remaining in that factory, in that forest, where the present was forlorn and the future was foreclosed. Today, when I don't want to do something, when resistance tries to keep me in the cocoon of comfort, I flashback to my origins—there is a rush of recall, and getting out of that bed sure is a lot easier.

ESCAPE

After nine months of choking on sawdust and lacquer, an avenue of escape became available. My parents delivered an ultimatum that engendered the quickest decision of my life. They offered to help send me to college, if and only if certain conditions were met. Before I heard the conditions, I said yes. It was a resounding yes. In life there is negotiation and then there is capitulation. The former is subject to the power to walk away; the latter is a surrender to the inevitable. I couldn't walk away from the offer—I capitulated without knowing the terms; it didn't matter. What the future held, I didn't know, but the present was something I could no longer endure. When there is no other option, risk is relative, it's all reward—I escaped from the fear of future life on a factory floor to the classrooms of higher education.

My metamorphosis from rebel without a clue to serious student of applied learning was framed in the context of forest, factory and the fear of a foreclosed future. Those past conditions that I endured became the fuel, the drive from fear, and the reason to escape. When people would walk in my dorm room at 2 A.M. and ask why I was studying when everyone else was partying, I told them I wasn't going back home, at least not from lack of unconditional effort. At that time I didn't know what I wanted, but I sure as hell knew what I feared—I knew what waited for me back in that town. The fear of going back drove me, possessed me, and propelled me forward to make the Dean's List and graduate with honors; education was the only way out, it was my lever from which to move my life forward.

BURN THE BOATS

When I think of the personal investment that defines total commitment in business, I am reminded of the actions taken by the leaders of the Greeks and Spanish conquistadors. Both the Greeks and Spaniards were geographically mandated to further their possessions by taking advantage of the sea. When they embarked upon land, the Greeks burned their boats and the Spaniards scuttled theirs. There was nothing behind them but the sea, no retreat. The only way to survive was to go forward, always forward.

When you adopt a no retreat mentality and bring your action into alignment with this thinking, you will personally invest, endure the sacrifice, and accept the challenge to overcome the obstacle, limit, or condition.

We need fear to remind us retreat is not an option, there is only one direction—forward. Insecurity and self-doubt can propel us from the depths of a deep internal need to validate our self-worth through accomplishment. Each of us must define accomplishment in our own terms. We seek the new car, work for the new home, and begin to clothe ourselves in a new wardrobe. Do we then begin to think and act as if success is a destination and we have arrived? Or, will we continue to strive to fulfill internal purpose as we gain external reward? Success is always under construction, it is a journey without end. We will be limited by society's valuation if we measure success externally or as an end in itself.

True happiness holds success as a process—a self-directed assessment of forward progress. People feel good about themselves when they make progress and engage in the type of work that has meaning to them beyond the external. Internal assessment, acceptance, and actualization of purpose is where true happiness resides.

"Everything can be taken from a man but one thing: the last of human freedoms—to choose one's attitude in any given set of circumstances, to choose one's own way."

— Viktor Frankl

The decision to commit will be one of the most vital choices you'll make in life. In order to do something well, you must make a commitment. If you don't commit in life and go all in, then you'll simply take what life gives you, and you'll earn what you deserve.

Before you commit, know the price of that commitment. Know what it is you're getting into and be willing to make the sacrifices to get the reward—emulate the Greeks and Spaniards and burn your boat!

FIND THE BIGGER FEAR

When I began my sales career, I used the perspective of my past to create the context for my present. My past consisted of rote work in a factory and the hard work of learning how to learn in college.

When things became difficult and the obstacles seemed insurmountable, I remembered the smells of sawdust and lacquer and it ignited a survival instinct within me. This instinct generated vivid images of my past that compelled my present activity to determine my future reality. I have found two distinct ways to overcome and move through fear. One is to find the challenge from a bigger fear, the other is to become connected to your purpose, compelled to do something from that deep well of internal conviction.

When we are compelled, we can move through the field of fear from the pull of purpose and meaning. When I entered the business arena I was uncertain. There were a lot of "no's" before I heard my first "yes!" I feared I would let the important people in my life down—those who had made opportunity available and championed my cause. I used fear for energy and made a commitment to myself that I embodied through action—I would do the work, extend the effort, and—by will, luck, or design—generate the result. I did not label my fear; in fact, I didn't even think of it as fear. I just thought it was a feeling, almost an extended adrenaline high that propelled me forward.

The more intense the need to succeed, the "must do"—the less significant the fear becomes. In the battle between compelling imperative and your biggest fear, victory will go to the strongest emotion. When your hunger compels you and you are dedicated, consumed with insatiable need, you will move away from the fields of fear. Once you start to move, you'll feel intrinsic gain as you realize the tangible progress that becomes the way forward.

ACTION STEPS

How do you know if you are ready to make the ultimate commitment and cross your personal Rubicon?

You are ready to cross your Rubicon if:

➔ Your compelling pull of purpose cannot be denied or quieted. There is a voice inside of you. It may start as a whisper and develop into a scream. It is a voice that begs to be heard. It will scream, "I must, I have to, I will." When the (compelling) voice is met with a pull from the gut (instinct), the alignment of the two—head and gut—means you're ready to cross your Rubicon.

➔ You have learned the cost of commitment; you are ready to make the sacrifice that is necessary to earn the reward.

➔ You have weighed all known factors. Be sure to evaluate your responsibilities with the known risks of the venture. Know that there will be sacrifices on both the home and business fronts. Strive to make a responsible and informed choice.

➔ The head will drive; the gut will govern. When both are in alignment, you're ready to go forward. When the head says yes and the gut feels calm, both at peace and in alignment, you're ready to go forward.

You're not ready to commit if:

→ You feel the tug of resistance in your gut. If your head informs, "But that's where the success is," and your gut feels uneasy and unsure, you are not ready. Remember: head and gut must be in alignment.

→ You're crossing just for the gold. Money is short-term motivation. Achievement demands a willingness to do what it takes to succeed. Sometimes motivation is not enough—what is required is inspiration. Inspiration comes from the depths of purpose. Inspiration is the internal fire that we have an obligation to find, stoke, and follow—it pulls us across the finish line. The energy of inspiration will lead you—the material will push you, purpose will pull you.

ALWAYS FORWARD: THE WAY THROUGH FEAR

T he neighborhood bullies were bored and on the lookout for prey. They chain-smoked cigarettes and guzzled beer and cheap wine. They stalked, much like the predators on the Savanna. Unlike the predators on the Savanna who survive by instinct, their lot was chosen.

That day, they found me. I was nine at the time.

As I would navigate the three-mile gauntlet to school every day from neighborhood to neighborhood, I was always vigilant of what lurked around corners.

The image from that day is still etched vividly in my mind. It changed the rest of my life from that day forward. I was wearing my prized birthday possession. I loved my brand new baseball hat with the small plastic baseball sewn on the front. The hat was cool because of that little ball on the front; it was unique, my favorite.

I can still remember those ornate, beveled stones that decorated the exterior of the church. There was a small enclave carved out of the façade. The bullies pounced from the shadows, the sounds of half-empty beer cans hitting pavement. The chase began. My legs were churning as I was running as fast as I could. I ran into the church enclave and was trapped. I remember the hat being torn off my head. Time was suspended and so was I, floating through the air from a shove, I watched the miniature baseball bounce around between those stones. There were laughs, taunts, threats, and anger in the faces and words of my tormentors.

I ran home, shirt torn, hat crumpled, the little baseball in my hand, my heart racing from the church all the way into my garage.

Working away in the garage was my father, a six-foot-three-inch authoritarian Pennsylvania State Police trooper. He was the county's version of John Wayne. As usual, he was covered in sawdust; wood working was his passion and pastime. He looked up and surveyed my torn and frayed clothing.

"Dad, Dad, they beat me up!"

My father leveled a serious look at me, then offered lecture and lesson. "Son, you can keep running from the bully, but one day you will run out of room. When you run out of room, you will have to make a choice. You can cower in the corner from fear, or you can stand, plant your feet, and face it."

That's life, we can run but at some point we will run out of room, grow tired, stop, and surrender. Life will present us with choices—we will either slink or cower in the shadow of fear, or take the pain and move forward. Each resolute step will make you stronger, forging your resolve and creating the self-confidence to move forward.

I began to build myself up, both mentally and physically. I learned to see my problems for what they were and faced them head-on. Over time, I developed an arsenal of resolve, fortitude, and spirit to dispatch the bullies in my life. Life will test our inner resolve. It will question, we must answer. We must be able to physically cash the checks our minds write.

The bullies in life—the big boys on the block—are fear, worry, and self-doubt. When we see them for what they are, fragments of our imagination that we project to be real, we can minimize them by facing them or run for the cover of the shadows. They will chase us. The more we run, the bigger they become. The bigger they become, the more difficult they are to overcome.

It's far more effective to draw fear and worry to the light than chase them from the shadows. When we stop fearing the shadows, we can take the first steps toward success. Bring your fears into the light of awareness—understanding can lead to the action that diffuses the energy of fear.

I owned the spirit of my father's message. From that point forward, I never ran again.

There will be times in life when conflict avoidance is a prudent strategy for survival. You can't fight all things at all times. Awareness of the physical and mental battles that are important to wage will dictate the outcomes of the wars you must win to move forward.

When avoidance morphs to resistance, the habits of delay and indecision can prevent or limit us from doing what is necessary and vital for our business and personal survival. We can see resistance in people. We watch as they slink into the cubicle. The phone stays in the cradle. The keys to the car stay in the desk, and they wait. They resist entering the field to overcome the dragon. They hesitate, and either the past or the present, the fear or the imagination, becomes the excuse, the condition, the unwillingness, and the end. One will never know until they are on the field, sword in hand or sword in scabbard. The dragon will be there, will you?

This is the paradox of fear—you must summon the courage to overcome the uncertainty that accompanies your need to feel safe. Humans harbor an instinct to resist the need for change and seek what they think is comfort in the safety of the known. Stepping forward, outside of your circle of comfort, is a risk. Choose to expand your horizon, learn more, apply what you learn and take intelligent risks that foster business and personal growth.

GET BACK UP

At the turn of the last century the great escape artist Harry Houdini began performing death defying escapes from straitjackets, jails, coffins, handcuffs, and shackles (defined as something that confines the arms or legs). At each performance he invited police officials onstage to examine him and his props to make sure they were real. In 1908, Houdini began performing a trick in which he was locked inside a large iron milk can filled with water. He could escape within three minutes. Here is what he had to say about fear:

> *Of fear I do not think—or courage. In the profession it is just habit—and nerve. Take a case. You are not frightened of falling from your feet; you balance on your feet. A good acrobat learns to balance on his head in just the same way. Then he will balance on his head on the top of a twenty-foot pole—easier there than on the ground, because you feel it sooner when you lose balance. Dangerous of course, and very few can do it. But those who can, they do not think of the danger; they began as little boys, and have practiced every day; it is habit.*

> *Then one day they fall—ah! That is the test—that is the courage. Always after that they have the thought of falling; it has never really come into their heads before. To face that thought, to fight it down, and do the trick—that is courage. And to do the trick knowing they will fall—*

because you must—because the audience is waiting—that is greater courage still. You feel the body shaking like a leaf, but your spirit drives it on.

THE FIRST STEP

Those ancestors of ours who took the first forward steps were bold. The progression of history is aligned with the nature of our species that expresses itself in forward motion. Life is a quest— our search will encounter adversity to engender growth. In our quest, we will live to the spirit of our cause, refine the raw pull of our purpose, and contain those self-defeating forces that impair, impede, or prevent the triumph from the quest.

"You will either step forward into growth, or you will step backward into safety."

— Abraham Maslow

The first step is the crucial step. Nothing can happen in life without the desire and the will to take the first step. As Neil Armstrong, the first man to step foot on the moon said, "This is one small step for man, one giant leap for mankind." It all started with that first step. The first step in facing fear is to locate its origin. May the journey begin.

A 30,000-FOOT PERSPECTIVE

Fear's pathway takes both a low road and a high road to the brain. The low road is instinct, and the high road is thought and analysis. The reptile brain is instinct. The limbic system houses our emotional pain and pleasure response, and the frontal cortex is our CEO brain of rational thought and logic. Our consciousness is our 30,000-foot perspective—when we get lost in a maze of analysis, we can become paralyzed by our own thoughts. Our awareness can bring a 30,000-foot perspective. We can see the maze for what it is and understand our obligation to act upon what we've learned.

THE UNFORGIVING ADVERSARY

Fear is a primitive response to a perceived threat. It can be a protective and adaptive ally or a limiting, unforgiving adversary. Fear is different than the threat of danger. Danger is a person or thing that is likely to cause harm or injury—fear can protect us from the danger inherent in the physical threats from the environment, enabling us to assess, anticipate, and act. The fear we will undress is not physical threat or harm—those dangers that spark our necessary survival mechanism—the instinctive protective system that can help us avoid a deranged person with a weapon or danger from a member of the animal kingdom, insect world, or reptile phylum. The emotion we will dissect is that invisible and insidious form that preys upon the imagination—

those pulse-quickening, confidence-eroding, imagined experiences that slow us down or stop us from pursuing dreams or creating our best life. The fear we must overcome is insidious; it weaves jealousy, anger, unworthiness, doubt, and shame through our psyche.

Past experiences spark the creation of imagined consequences in the future. One must find the courage to avoid looking back through the past darkly. Our imagination can magnify those things that have happened in the past and project them vividly into the future. Often, the worst-case scenario never occurs, and if it does, it rarely matches the mind's potential for florid, catastrophic imagined scenarios.

HARDWIRED

Our social fears are also linked to our ancestors. Survival on the plains of the Savanna was contingent upon the help of the tribe. If we were ostracized, we weren't safe. Researchers believe human babies are born with just two innate fears: the fear of falling and the fear of loud noises. All other fears are socially learned. The brain's primary function is to provide for our survival and this mechanism is hardwired into our DNA. The genetic code passed on to us from our ancestors provides fear's gift in the flight, fight or freeze response. Instincts rule and compress the distance between an image and the perception of threat. We have a feral instinct that senses danger. The alarm of stress response is interpreted by the amygdala through our neural transmitters.

Fear has evolved from our primal function of anticipation and the avoidance of physical pain to the anticipation and avoidance of mental pain. We suffer self-imposed injuries to the ego, psyche, undergo humiliation, experience sorrow, and reflect in regret. We dread our mental anguish, yet we embrace the conditions that foster it.

So, we can thank our parents, teachers, friends, and foes for our socially learned fears. We can thank our ancestors on the Savanna for our resistance to the uncertain, those unseen or unforeseen elements of change. Since our social fears are learned, they can, by degree, be unlearned. To do so you must summon the willingness to expose yourself to those fears in order to lessen their impact. You will find that nothing in life worthy of merit can be accomplished without first moving through your dominant fears.

FERRARI, PRIUS, OR PORSCHE?

Imagine primitive man waking up to a shiny, new red 458 Ferrari Italia parked next to him. Would he look over and wonder if his neighbor was parking a Prius or Porsche in his cave? Would he even see the car? Or if he did, would he perceive it to be a threat? Would he become startled and try to fight it, or would he flee? If instinct compelled him to fight, that would be one expensive repair job on the 458. His ability to grasp the concept of a car extends beyond his comprehension. The ancient brain could not rationally process information—it could only respond based on instinct. Ironically, modern humans continue to be subject to the initial instinct of the ancient brain in the modern world—a brain that is incompatible with the iPads, electric cars, and futuristic orientation of today.

THE SABER-TOOTHED TIGER OF TODAY

In the days of our ancestors, the fight-or-flight system protected us from saber-toothed tigers. I've travelled the world extensively, and I've yet to come across a saber-toothed tiger. So where do the saber-toothed tigers exist in today's world? They exist in rush hour traffic, when we miss a deadline, have an argument with a spouse or lover, and put ourselves under extreme stress. The activations of hormones from toxic stress flow through our bodies from a perceived threat. This activation and release is no longer designed to protect us from physical danger on the Savanna. Awareness and choice have become our weapons against the saber-toothed tigers of today. When we are conscious of what is happening, we can choose to contain the spread of fear by understanding and then attempting to relieve the tension through our awareness.

STICK OR SNAKE?

The slightly more advanced part of the brain is the limbic system; it associates behaviors with agreeable or disagreeable experiences. Our limbic brain is home to emotional anchors and the primal needs of hunger, pain, fear, anger, pleasure, and sleep. This system allows us to make value judgments based on past experiences—it is the part of the brain that is associated with our emotions.

Can you avoid that flight-or-fight feeling when you sense danger? Can you tell your heart to stop beating? The emotional field of the limbic brain sends signals of caution when you encounter negative associations with past experiences of fear. But the most recently evolved part of the brain, the neocortex, is subject to plasticity—which means additional neuron development and therefore increased learning skill. The neocortex can bring reason into the equation. Reason will not eliminate that initial instinctual impulse—it's too strong—but it can help to understand and navigate the primal urge. It is what allows us to make the distinction between stick and snake. It is the thoughtful interpreter of information. The deeper we submerge into understanding what's happening, the more capable we will become of dissecting that fear response for what it is, allowing us to face it, deal with it, and move through it.

OUR CEO BRAIN

We need instinct and reason to function; we need to know when to employ instinct and when to override the lizard's scream. This part of our brain, referred to as the "executive brain," is where we differentiate among thoughts through reason. It is our rational sorting system. But when the amygdala—the source of fear-response in the brain—screams to the hypothalamus, creating the chemical ooze that generates instinct, releasing those stress hormones like cortisol, we can, with some effort, take a step back and think "What's going on here?" "Are my thoughts warranted?" Remember, this is outside of the danger zone—if we see a poisonous snake or a man with a knife, we are subject to the instinctual. Our instincts are designed to keep us safe. Our prefrontal cortex brings rationality into the process and allows us to differentiate between stick and snake.

- Fear is an indicator of what we must do to improve, grow, and flourish.

- Fear distracts us by redirecting our attention to previous endeavors that may have ended in failure. It deceives us by pointing out others who have tried and come up short in the pursuit that we now embark upon.

- Fear uses outcomes in our past to make its point in the present. That lizard brain screams to us, "You can't, you'll fail!"

- Fear creates the illusion of negative outcome and keeps us shuddering in that circle of comfort we create from the familiar.

- Fear turns our imagination loose on us—it runs rampant through our minds, projecting today's set-back as tomorrow's self-fulfilling prophecy of defeat.

- "Fear takes us further than we want to go and keeps us

longer than we want to stay."—Dr. Rob Bell, *No Fear:
A Simple Guide to Mental Toughness.*

THE DECISION BEHIND THE DECISION

There are two dominant fears: the fear of loss and the fear of change. Before anyone buys your expansive portfolios, persuasive proposals, or sterling products, know what you face—you face their fears. You're not only facing the competition—you're facing your prospects' fear of loss as well as their fear of change.

Here's the stuff they don't teach you in grad school: A person in a position to choose you as a vendor or partner already has risk involved in the decision. A bad decision can cause them not only loss of face but also loss of power, position, title, and perhaps, job. People pick brand names and well-known products because those choices are safe. There is a safety in numbers, a comfort in conformity with the masses. In those early days on the Savanna if you were ostracized from the masses, you were in peril and subject to death from the elements or the beasts that roamed on the free range.

Some people select safe because it is in their nature to safeguard their interests with a known choice. Even if they realize a distinct advantage, they may choose the comfort of the known. I learned that one will rarely hear the fear in other people, but their behavior will point to its origin. Your first sale is to the other person's fears. If you wish to explore the science behind this dynamic, I cite Daniel Kahneman who posits, "People are loss averse. When confronted with a decision they will err on the side of unreasonable caution rather than cope with a possible loss. They may ignore the big picture, and the result is a timid decision that can lead to mistakes just as surely as optimism can."

Remember, we fear change and we prefer safety. Known mediocrity is often the select choice for those who fear risk and are change averse. Those who do not like change tolerate the familiar, even if their perception of a superior partner or product may indicate a level of significant improvement over their current situation. If we focus on the competition instead of enrolling the buyer to move forward, we are missing the point of engagement, expending energy and effort chasing useless distraction. Distractions are like the cape to the bull in a bullfight. The bull follows the cape but gets killed by the sword. The sword is the words, action, and perhaps inaction we ignore. The sword is the behaviors we rationalize, or the unwillingness to face, make and implement the choices from life's difficult decisions. We can distract ourselves from the purpose at hand, but at some point, we must face the consequences of our distractions.

RESISTANCE CHECKPOINT

Ask yourself, if fear didn't stop you, what would you do today? The answer will determine the quality of your tomorrow.

Before we can get to yes, we have to anticipate and address the prospects' fears. If you don't address their fears, you won't get to yes—you might get to maybe, but maybe doesn't cash the checks. Choose not to focus predominantly on what the competition is doing. If we focus solely on the competition, we'll get jabbed by the sword. Start looking for the sword and ignore the cape.

In life, like, kind and quality often seeks like, kind and quality. We often get the clients we deserve. Attempt to engage those with intellectual curiosity, a strong ethical backbone, a high degree of fairness, and a willingness to take some risks. Improve your knowledge base, expand your intellectual curiosity, hone your empathy, and increase your listening skills to the degree that what a person says is what you hear, as opposed to hearing what you wish them to say. Earn self-esteem and exhibit it. Choose to work with those who appreciate your value.

Other than a one-time sale of a product, relationship selling is a process. Choose not to lurch or grab for something, but assume and position yourself in such a way as to not look desperate or needy. Prospects expect us to convince, cajole, coerce or push them toward our product, service or platform.

Take a different approach for positive impact. Restrain the urge to rush the process, deflect the immediacy of having to make the sale now—push them away. When I practiced a subtle "push-away," nine out of ten times they pulled me back and said "Well, maybe this year is the year". I wasn't in it for the quick buck, fast sale. I have found that often the harder and longer it takes to court and win the heart of a client, the greater the duration of the relationship. I have also found the opposite to be true. If a sale comes too easily, it often goes away just as fast and easy. Any port in the storm will do when all you sell is price and you're willing to give up your self-respect to gain a short-term deal.

This is not a tactic or approach, it is a way. The effectiveness of this "way" is contingent upon the amount and quality of suspects you are building through your directed activity. You must always build, cultivate, and engage in activity that expands your base of suspects. Your ability to qualify suspects into prospects and apply the lessons of enrollment outlined in this book will improve your chances of turning prospects into clients. The desperate are those who have little in the system—few suspects, and even fewer prospects. Those who have to make every sale to survive end up making very few or none.

People are not attracted to desperate, needy or greedy. People are attracted to success. They want to do business with those they perceive to be a source of value.

TELLING FEAR TO GO TO HELL

I find Winston Churchill's wit and wisdom to be both enlightening and inspiring. His quotes always provide a burst of inspiration—the depth of insight is underscored by his particular brand of sarcastic wit. Depending upon your political slant and understanding of history, you may think the wartime prime minister was either the savior of Western civilization or the embodiment of self-aggrandizement and the epitome of the truism that the winners write history. When visiting London, I like to tour the Churchill War Rooms—a part of the Imperial War Museums that exhibit the actual wartime bunker that sheltered Churchill and his government during the Blitz. If you visit London and you have a passing interest in history, the Imperial War Museum is a must see. As I walked into the museum, I saw this quote flashed upon a screen:

> Success is not final, failure is not fatal: it is the courage to continue that counts.

Against what seemed like insurmountable odds and an enveloping despair in Britain, Churchill, through will, resolve, and the ability to ignore fear, rallied a country against what was at the time, the greatest fear: Nazi Germany. His legendary walks home to 10 Downing Street during the height of bombing raids were his metaphorical middle finger thrust out to Hitler. He didn't just face fear; he told fear to go to hell!

OUR MENTAL MAPQUEST

Fear continues to enable our survival. The source of instinct that protected our ancestors yesterday remains our formidable ally today. Fear plots a navigational course for our lives. Even the smallest of fears, if they seep into our mental MapQuest, can take us off course. Fear can help us navigate the world, but it also can limit our experience of it. When fear consumes us, we cede control to our old brain and revert to the behavioral mode that was critical to past survival. The reptile brain dominates our impulsive action and attempts to negate intellect and will. If it succeeds, we succumb to the instinctual sway of evolution's earliest dawn.

The dragon of fear prefers the shield of darkness, the edges of the nocturnal, the solitude of our company, and the dark, where the dragon's breath is unleashed as worry, doubt, and insecurity. The dragon seeks to confine and isolate you—to make your imagination an adversary, instead of your creative ally. The dragon seeks to make you fear loss and uncertainty. It wants you to cower in the shelter of conformity and avoid change. One day from the shadows of the cave, one will emerge. Will it be you or the dragon?

Fear will erode our spirit; it is insidious, a virus of the mind—it weakens our resolve of spirit and blocks the forward path of progress. Fear will produce a life of fatigue. As the ancient sage Pliny the Younger is reputed to have said, "Grief has limits, whereas apprehension has none. For we grieve only for what we know has happened, but we fear all that possibly may happen." When we fear for our future, we foreclose our present. Believe life is worth living—the belief can propel inspired action. Inspired action can create favorable conditions for success. Your progress will be subject to the sway of your imagined fears and your willingness to do the work it takes to move forward.

What you say to yourself will be reflected outwardly and affect others. Telling yourself that you can't do it means you won't. Telling yourself it is too difficult means it will be. Telling yourself you aren't good enough means you believe that you're not. And telling yourself it can wait means that someone is doing today what you intend to do tomorrow. Self-talk and understanding reflect what you think and do. You will lessen the impact of fear when you hold it up to the light, view it for the invisible barrier that it is, and contain its limiting power by taking action!

Experience and feeling can become the arbiter between rush and procrastination. Some will think and then wait, maybe think some more, delay, and then when they think the stars are aligned, perhaps do something.

Begin a small journal, a calendar, specifically outlining your fear. Perhaps you fear making phone calls, or delivering presentations, maybe speaking in public, or approaching a potential date. Whatever it is, write it down, but before you do, remember the commitment you made when you crossed your personal Rubicon. You have to move forward and do those things that you fear—perhaps not all in one leap, but in incremental steps. You won't overcome the fear of presentations in a few runs, but your preparation and self-confidence will grow when you learn there is no saber-toothed tiger in the conference room.

LIGHT IT UP

Keep in mind the difference between those fears that are an inevitable consequence of life and those that are imagined experiences in the future. You can fear death, but whether you fear it or not, just like everyone else, your time on Earth will one day end. You can fear making presentations, but to avoid doing them is the death of business. Be willing to accept the uncomfortable for what it is, a rite of passage, and a chance for growth. Every day you take that step forward, you move further from the fear you wrote in your calendar and closer to the goals you write down every morning. Let a week pass—a week of your willingness to face fear—then look back on what you wrote in the calendar. It may now seem insignificant, and you will find that in most cases it has less power over you than it once did. You can apply the same technique with fear's cousin, worry. When you look at that page and you feel that you have overcome the fear, tear it out, put a match to it, and watch it burn. You will feel much better for the experience. You will gain strength each time you perform the exercise. Life is to move forward, always forward. Come up from the basement of fear and light it up!

When your light is extinguished, will the difference you made in life extend beyond your time on earth? Did you make a difference for others by first making a difference for yourself—facing, containing, controlling, and overcoming fear?

A friend of mine, Perry Thomas Chapman, crafted a book of legacy for his family. In it, he said something I think is beautiful, profound, and answerable only through the passing of time: "Random thoughts on my life are not definable. I am not sure if my life will leave permanent marks or will pass in obscurity, like the contrails of a high flying aircraft." The answer will be found in the people we mentor who will create their legacy from the lessons, teaching, and example we offer in the present.

Face a dominant fear today—it will help you overcome lesser fears tomorrow. I don't know if it's possible to overcome all of our fears; fear is, after all, a part of our DNA and our ever-present immersion in our social surroundings. But if we understand the nature of our fear and see it for the impotent instrument of our imagination that it is, we can take the steps to face it and overcome its limiting nature.

ACTION STEPS

→   Know the difference between fear and danger. Fear is a primitive response to a perceived threat. It can be a protective and adaptive ally or a limiting, unforgiving adversary. Fear is different from danger. Danger is a person or thing that is likely to cause harm or injury.

→ Find the resolve to face your fear. Each time you face fear, you can gain strength of confidence and build experience. Confidence and experience can foster courage.

→ Stop feeding your fear. Learn what you can and can't influence and control in life. Limit the imagination's default to worst-case scenario. Take the necessary steps to achieve the best possible outcome. Remember: we consume messages, verbal and nonverbal cues every day from the time we flip on the television in the morning until we retire into the dark recesses of night. Be aware and make a choice to limit and understand the dynamic. Act accordingly.

→ Gain traction, move forward, visualize, and become more than the sum of your fears. The experienced reality of your fears is rarely as bad as what you've imagined. Facing fear will be uncomfortable, it may hurt, you may feel like stopping, you might even pause for a while, but you must never quit.

→ Remember: we choose to recall and construct our good and bad experiences from the narrative of memory. If we anchor our present position to a negative past experience, we may avoid the change that can positively impact our future. When we are aware of this selective conditioning, we can adjust and adapt.

➜ Fail fast, fail often, learn always. The pantheon of success is littered with the vestiges of failure.

➜ Preparation lowers the fear threshold. Prepare by learning and growing self-confidence– anticipate, learn, and apply.

➜ Attempt to assess and understand the situation for what it is, not what you wish it to be. Picture yourself stepping outside of the situation and reframing the way you view it. Frame it in context. Does this have an immediate or long-range implication in the quality of your life or doesn't it?

➜ Don't fight ghosts. We create more issues from the anxiety of assumption than we are ever forced in reality to battle. Ghosts are those things we assume or imagine to have a power or presence. We can't physically fight our assumptions or imagination, but we can become aware that we are engaged in a struggle we have created in our mind. Awareness can bring perspective and can prevent us from chasing the limiting shadows cast from our imagination.

PART II

THE SEVEN SECRETS OF SALES SUCCESS

"There is no moment like the present. The man who will not execute his resolutions when they are fresh upon him can have no hope from them afterwards: they will be dissipated, lost, and perish in the hurry and scurry of the world, or sunk in the slough of indolence."

— Maria Edgeworth

ACTIVITY RULES SUCCESS

"**A**ctivity Rules Success"—it was inscribed on a ruler in the drawer of a bullpen desk. The contents of the desk contained the ruler, a paperclip, and a dull #2 pencil. The remnants were the parting gifts left to me from someone who had just been terminated. I guess that person didn't measure up to the expectations outlined in the sales quota. The rulers, I thought, were the company's action statement or the consequences for lack thereof.

"Activity Rules Success" is the essential guiding mantra that has forged my way in business for the past three decades. I live this statement as a personal truth and guiding light—a mantra, a maxim; it is much more than a resonant phrase. This rule gave direction and life to opportunity through action. Through action, I attracted and earned those things that gave me a better standard of living. I knew if I couldn't outthink I'd have to outwork and if I was outworked, well, that was on me. I may be outsmarted, but the opponent had to pack a lunch and dinner. I wasn't going away. It was all day, every day. Stoke the fire in the belly—be hungry for success.

Each of us has an internal work thermostat—you know when you put in a full day, when you extend yourself and put in every ounce of focused energy to get the result. You also know when you waste time and expend energy on useless tasks just to fill the day. You can observe this in the workplace every day. Some people take four hours of work and turn it into an eight-hour day. Some people take eight hours of work, turn it into a four-hour day and then find more work to fill the day and create opportunity. This is both mindset and work ethic—one of the differences between those who succeed and those who just want a job, a paycheck, and a way to survive.

There are two resources that drive and govern our decisions. One is logic, the other, emotion. They are often not in concert; one may pull or drive as the other cautions and resists. When I started in business, I had an unyielding conviction and belief in myself. I thought, "What's the commonality in any business?" It's people. People were going to buy the product. I wanted responsibility at the point of sale; I wanted to be a difference maker. If activity would govern my success, I was going to generate the type of activity that would make this happen. I think you can find motivation from what you fear, or from what you must have to survive. You must survive before you can thrive; fear fueled my need to achieve and drove me forward.

Whatever the guidelines or rule of thumb for success in your industry, you must do more. Meeting minimum expectations delivers subpar results. Quotas are guidelines for average, and average doesn't create expansive lifestyle options.

There are books floating around in business that suggest you do multiples of ten times the expected or minimum. I don't know if the rule applies for every industry, but I do know that the amount of activity that you put in—intelligent, directed effort conducted at a brisk but measured pace—will generate more access to potential clients. The more potential clients you meet, the more prospects you can qualify and enroll as customers.

Your customer base is your most potent selling machine. The more extensive and influential your customer base, the more credible and powerful your perceived talents and realized capabilities. Your daily activity is where it starts. Activity grows your client base, but not before you do the work to earn your client list one customer at a time.

"How do you eat an elephant?" is the first part of an Ethiopian proverb. The answer is "One bite at a time." In retrospect, most have to overcome difficulties to arrive at their current station. To look back can be overwhelming. It can also be encouraging. The message on the ruler resonated with me emotionally. It made sense logically. "Activity Rules Success." To own a statement as fact and translate fact to action and consistent result, you have to own it and use it, you have to be emotionally attached to it.

THE RAW-TO-REFINED EXPRESSIVE—
HOW TO PUT PASSION, PURPOSE, AND PULSE INTO A BUSINESS LETTER

Business letters aren't often used as a forum to move people, but rather, as an insipid platform that underscores and often painfully outlines directives, requests, and static concepts. Do you want to move people with your writing? Then put some passion into your prose. Make the words flow from thought to page and animate the image your words attempt to convey.

Here's how to start: generate a thought from an image that moves you emotionally. Close your eyes and just focus on the image, and then with as little thought as possible, start to write those feelings that best describe that emotional connection. Let it flow in raw form. Scribble thoughts and words; forget about structure. Forget about style, and just let the writing flow. Picture a large easel, not a legal-sized tablet. After you express your feeling, look to apply the logic of thought to anchor your emotional proposition.

People connect to emotion. People are moved by emotion. People are emotional beings who are influenced and make most decisions at the emotional level. When decisions are made at the subconscious level or even conscious level of emotion, people use logic to support or validate their emotional decision.

Make your words come to life. You win hearts by pouring yourself into and becoming the message. The best of life comes from engagement, active participation, finding the sweet spot, locating the marrow of the bone. Cold science is a tool for dissection—emotion is the art and gift of intersection with people.

Express the essence of what you feel, and then refine it. Use the raw, expressive, free flow of emotion, and then refine and frame it with logic. Let those feelings flow to the page. When you come to an impasse, take a short break, think about something else, and then come back to it. Look over your writing and think of how those words support what you want to say. Think of how you are going to frame them and why you are going to use them in your talk or correspondence. It is more effective to begin with a raw form and then refine it. It is very difficult, if not impossible, to make the refined raw.

We sometimes push words to the page as we attempt to generate enlightened answers, make the ideal sales pitch or form persuasive argument. When we do so, we often miss the important elements of enthusiasm, energy, and the feeling that provides the connection between writer and intended audience. It is easier to take feeling out of the page then it is to insert it into a logical treatise. Logic is a product of rational thought; feeling is the expression of emotion. The duality of their force trumps a singular approach that treats logic and emotion as mutually exclusive.

Just let the prose go with flow and feeling. Don't think. You can then apply logic to supply the anchors to the emotional flow from the words that create feeling.

FAILING FORWARD

We all have to start somewhere. When I started my career, I was shipped-off to training courses for nine months. Everything that was taught in a formulaic approach confused me. It interfered with my focused listening and desire to be pulled through the portal of another person's experience so I could learn about them and find a way, if there was one, to work with them. I found my style to be antithetical to the stay-on-script order taker. I was unsuccessful in my first thirteen attempts to generate yes. Each failure brought me closer to success. I thought, "I just need to get in front of more people to win my first sale." I was failing forward, I was learning how to do it, I was getting closer each time. I applied what I learned. I didn't feel fear. I felt myself acting in alignment with the message on the ruler. I never lost heart or the flame of self-belief, I owned the thought every day that if it was to be, it was up to me.

Originality gains attention because it's different, and it makes a difference because it's original. The same approach that solved yesterday's problems may not be the best analytical or emotional set of tools in today's fluid, change-by-the-minute environment.

EGO WITH ABILITY IS TALENT, EGO WITHOUT TALENT IS ARROGANCE

I was learning the streets and flying to different cities to sit in classrooms. Which activity do you think I preferred? Class was boot camp for the uninitiated rookie. On the first day of class, the instructor looked around the room with the dispassionate delivery of an automaton, and made us aware of the percentages of people who made it past the nine-month period. He said, and I paraphrase, that if we looked to our left and to our right, both of those people will be gone. It is one out of three that make it.

Fear was palpable in the room. I looked around and thought, *Man I really like this guy on my left and the girl on my right is cool too. I'm going to miss them.* I had my guiding message; activity was going to rule my success, and I was just going to keep going, going, and going. The dragon of fear may have warmed the room with its fiery breath, but it had nothing on the fear of going back to the furnace and forge of my youth.

Fear is an imagined or anticipated event in the future that we perceive as real. Imagination will work for or against us. We need our imagination to visualize what it is we want and how we will feel when we obtain it. Left unchecked, imagination will run into the shadows of fear and expand them until they stifle us. The stronger our need, want, and desire, our must-have, the weaker the hold fear will have over our imagination.

Let's revisit the percentages and statistics that rule
this jungle of survive-or-perish. It is important to note that
statisticians use statistics much like a drunk uses a lamp post—
for support, not proof. Imagination will work for or against us.

- To avoid being a statistic, know that activity rules
  success. This is raw and direct, not precise and
  accurate. I prefer raw and direct.

- Find a way or make a way—your corporate survival
  may just depend on it. Those with a yes bias find a way
  to make things happen.

- The success of your activity will be reflected by your
  willingness to face your fear, bring it to light, and
  undress it for what it is—an imagined expectation.

- Learn to prepare for the worst case scenario. Don't
  expect it, but explore options that provide contingency
  plans. Know your downside and manage it. Imagined
  fear can act as the grizzly bear in our lives. We may
  expect the bear to appear, but it often doesn't. Prepare
  to meet the bear, but don't become obsessed with the
  potential downside of a remote occurrence. (Remote
  does not apply to those people living in Canada or
  Alaska.) Most of the time the bear never shows.
  Balance your assessment of current reality by learning
  of and preparing for, the potential downside of risk.

- The saying "experience is the best teacher" is only applicable if the student learns and applies the lesson. If she doesn't, it is just an experience.

RESISTANCE CHECKPOINT

Is your activity focused and directed, or are you engaged in efforts that distract or detract you from your goal?

When I learned of the percentages and looked around the room, I didn't know what anyone else was thinking or what images crossed their mind. However, brown-bag bologna sandwiches and the smell of sawdust and lacquer fueled the survival instinct within me—that instinct that generated vivid images of my past; those images that compelled my present activity to determine my future reality, a reality that would determine my future by the activity that would rule my success.

I've found one of the ways to overcome and move through a fear is to find the motivation from a bigger fear. My biggest fear in this timeframe was letting significant others down—those who had made opportunity available and championed my cause. I used fear for energy and made a commitment to myself that I embodied through action. I would do the work, extend the effort, and by will, luck, or design generate the result. I did not label my fear—I thought it was just part of the challenge that moving forward presented.

I was determined to become a difference-maker. Difference-makers alter the equation in their favor by changing the dynamic and influencing the result. They make a difference through their presence, personality, product knowledge, and applied people skills. They roll-up their sleeves and work. Their work is a passionate pursuit that comes from that deep well of meaning that is unique to each individual. When we discover what it is that we must have, we will find or make a way to realize the experience or achieve the result. If we are to realize achievement every day, we must live to the spirit of our promise. Achievement is an incremental process that demands mastery, practice, patience and application. We must fight through every disappointment and enjoy each success. Every turn, bump, and climb on the road will, for some, become the journey worth taking.

ACTION STEPS:

→ Be aware that there is no magic elixir or silver bullet that creates success without work. Are you willing to do the work? If you combine intellect with people skills and what your industry recognizes as ability, you have a chance to move forward. Your activity will rule the opportunities you make available from the concentrated energy you expend with directed purpose.

→ Are you ready to show up and engage in the focused activities that will separate you from the field? If Activity Rules Success, will you do what it takes to succeed? Many opportunities in life are realized by people who just show up. Those who show up compelled to engage in purposeful activity with resolve of purpose and clarity of message make things happen. Learn what distractions are and choose to avoid them— work on the things that make a difference.

→ Find your inner artist—be creative—think of methods and ideas that come from inside and outside the company. Don't overlook the obvious but try to imagine solutions that create opportunities for your advancement.

→ Always be open to learn—ask questions, seek the answers. If you can't find the answers, strive to create the best possible solution—own it, become it, and do it. We can learn from our own mistakes or the mistakes of others—which do you prefer? In your march to progress, you will learn the difference between activity that leads to intended result and unfocused energy expenditure that leads to frustration. When I became aware of the time I wasted doing that which was inconsequential, I applied what I learned and adjusted accordingly.

THINK AND DO

T hink and do, you'll be far ahead of those who don't and won't. The shorter the time lapse between deliberate thought and purposeful, directed activity, the greater the likelihood of success in the endeavor. The inverse is also true. Think and do is the essential element for success at any level of engagement. Here's why—success is the product of forward motion—it is the marriage of deliberate thought and decisive action. Instinct and thought is static; action is dynamic. For instance, Isaac Newton sat on his bed with his feet on the floor, deep in thought. He did this for hours. But unless he actually put pen to paper, his thoughts were just that, inner workings of the imagination and the expansion of critical thought. Without action Newton may not have brought forth calculus, which, in my opinion would have been a good thing.

To think and then do affects separation and embodies distinction. Here's why—many people think but choose not to do. They ruminate and contemplate. Some people do without thinking. This is blindly ambitious at best, misguided and reckless at worst. Later in this chapter, there is an example of Custer's folly and his rash, impudent action without thought. Here's a spoiler alert: it didn't end well. When instinct encourages thought, and thought follows action, we initiate the advantages of forward motion and momentum.

"Failures are divided into two classes—those who thought and never did and those who did and never thought."
— John Charles Salak

There is a power in the simplicity of think and do, a challenge in its consistent execution, and a definite difference in the result from its applied action. Think and do will move your value proposition forward. Most will be playing catch-up to your lead. Don't wait for the call, make the call. Get out and press flesh. Choose not to become one who remains captive to the resistance of fear. Choose not to be the apathetic one, unwilling to do what it takes to win the day. Maintain the sovereignty of the self and take responsibility for your personal product.

Fear can prevent action and limit our field of thought. We remain in our circle of comfort, waiting for someone to call us, or we overthink and attempt to perfect our approach. We succumb to the pull of resistance. Resistance will hold us in our seats and prevent us from taking the action necessary to move our proposition forward. In the extensive literature on the subject of fear, we can reduce most of the jargon, concept, and scientific study to one thing—action. We must face our fears. That's right; to move forward in life, we must face our fears. Follow your instinct with thought and your thought with action. You will find that by doing so, the forward motion of action will release your imagination from the throes of fear.

"Fear stifles our thinking and actions. It creates indecisiveness that results in stagnation. I have known talented people who procrastinate indefinitely rather than risk failure. Lost opportunities cause erosion of confidence and the downward spiral begins."

– Charles Stanley

Let's imagine you are leaving a prospect or client's office. You had what you think is the most fantastic, earth-shattering, sweet-spot, home-run, crushing call of all. (Salespeople worth their salt think most of their calls are fantastic.)

It's the optimism gene, the one that keeps you going when failure is always one call away. Let's say you have this feeling that maybe you should call, just to thank the person again for the meeting; you've already sent a thank-you email, thanking him for his time and consideration while highlighting the key talking points and action items for the next meeting. But, instinct compels you to call just to thank him for the pleasure of his acquaintance.

Remember, the safe instinct, the reptile brain, seeks to avoid the scrutiny and embarrassment of rejection. It seeks safe. We need to summon the prefrontal cortex, use the fire power of will, take a deep breath, and make the call. By making the call, you'll begin to separate yourself from the field of potential suitors. Make the call!

My mental picture of sales is a transaction, while my image of enrollment is a process that is founded upon relationship. When we engage from the heart, enrollment begins. Enrollment is sales on steroids; it is strong and binding. Enrollment is different from sales. It's more than just semantics— mindset directs the behavior that makes the difference.

Enrollment is recruitment. When we enroll, we engage hearts and minds, not the purse. Enrollment aligns agenda and motive, revealing strengths, weaknesses and opportunities in both parties' platforms. Enroll others through authenticity, transparency and realized value. Earn the right to become the buyer's choice. Believe in your product, your teammates, and yourself. Believe with conviction that you are the best choice to serve another person's needs—make it personal. Making it personal requires an emotional investment. People feel emotion when it is authentic and imbued with self-belief. Emotion is what creates enrollment. Logic simply supports the choice.

In the traditional sales model, prospects expect to be sold. Have the moxie to flip the model. Become distinctive by choosing to be open and transparent; enroll from the heart. Enrollment is a process; think and do is a part of that process. People want to know you care about them before they care about what you know. Use your head and gut, don't swarm someone, hone your gift of feeling, and know when and how to subtly stay on their radar screen.

Enrollment is sitting side by side with another, not across the table, sometimes literally but always figuratively. Enrollment aligns agenda and motive and reveals strengths, weaknesses, and opportunities in both parties' platforms.

If you are to maintain momentum, you have to stay on the other person's radar screen. You'll have to judge the timing of your approach on an individual-by-individual basis. There's a point between being a pain in the posterior and taking the incremental steps toward partnership by staying present and engaged. Remember, first and foremost, incremental steps forward win the day, the deal, the month, the quarter, the year. They also define the quality of your career. If you attempt to close too quickly, it will be very difficult to overcome that initial no. It is better to move forward on solid ground from feel, instinct, and logic, than to try to fly to yes without permission to take off.

Prepare, plan and execute to achieve the small wins that will move you forward! In football, a first down is comprised of ten yards. A first down rewards a team with four more plays to make another ten yards. If they make or exceed the ten yards, they earn another first down. Plays that generate a positive gain move the chains (the measuring system for ten yards). First downs move the team closer to the goal line. When you try for big plays too early it may lead to quarterback sacks, penalties, loss of yardage, and a longer distance to the next first down. In business this is asking for the order too quickly, or, getting careless and assuming you're at step five in your qualifying process when in reality you're at step two. Rookie mistakes are painful emotionally, less so physically, than in the NFL. In both business and football, it can be very difficult to recover from an early setback. Losses screw up your rhythm, take you out of your practiced approach or preferred system, and they make you take chances. Incremental wins make first downs, each play every day, must move you toward yes—each engagement, each conversation must move your value proposition forward. It must move you closer to the goal you seek.

The game of sales is about field position and maintaining momentum, moving forward, knowing when to go deep and when to play for first downs. There is an art to this—I am a deep throwing quarterback, I want to go deep on every play. I like the challenge of third and long. But I've learned that to risk on first down requires knowledge of the proper time, place, and position on the field to go for it all. Experience and listening skills will dictate when to go for more than the first down. Listen with your head to what the other person says and don't let arrogance or assumed skill get in the way of progress.

Our instincts are designed to keep us safe and they do so by resisting change and avoiding loss. Our rational sorting system, our CEO brain can help us decide when to take that risk and when it is unwise or unhealthy to do so. When we are aware that we need to do something and face a fear, we can make the choice, become compelled to do so, and use willpower to propel us forward, through fear.

Willpower is finite, but it can be developed. I will show you how in a later section. Be cautious not to spend too much time thinking about a perfect approach, the perfect strategy, the perfect action plan. If you strive for perfection, you run the risk of waiting while others do the taking.

FORTUNE FAVORS THE BOLD

"Fortune favors the bold," Napoleon is credited to have proclaimed. Even those who dare, the ones who feel the tug of instinct, think, and act, feel the fear. What they do with the fear, how they assess it, and how they move in spite of it, is what makes their air rarified and their results consistent. They link their understanding of fear's limits to the growth demands that their courage invokes to overcome the resistance, the dragon, the shadow. They have a non-negotiable obligation to achieve that contributes to one of the differences in the quality of their life. Delay is a consequence of fear and it is severe. If you delay, you run the risk of waiting while others do the taking. The fortunes, the rewards, go to those who risk intelligently and move audaciously.

"Commitment is what transforms a promise into reality. It is the words that speak boldly of your intentions and the actions which speak louder than words. It is making time when there is none; coming through time after time, year after year. Commitment is the stuff that character is made of, the power to change the face of things. It is the daily triumph of integrity over skepticism."

— Abraham Lincoln

I am more adamant, passionate, and convinced of this connectivity between thought and action as the difference maker, the essential action that bridged the forest of my past to the beach of my present, than any concept I could offer. The successful think and do it now. If you aspire to be in the top tier of your industry, make think and do a habit that becomes your style, signature and way. Think and do is a learned habit that will summon the gift of instinct into the realm of thought. It will help you take the best course of action to deliver and separate you and your product from the competition.

Exceptional is, by definition, that which is above the ordinary, separate from the pack. Success is an individual proposition—no amount of coaching, cajoling, or other means of persuasion can substitute for that innate drive and unyielding will to succeed. I have found these traits to be common and shared among proven winners in various fields of endeavor. They consistently exhibit these traits and seek to eclipse the previous standards that they establish for themselves.

- They don't work from 9:00 a.m. to 5 p.m.

- When they work, they really work. They don't pretend or play

- They play to their strengths, be it personality or product knowledge

- They take ownership of the company's sales system and become the embodiment of its philosophy and process. Their unique personal immersion in the system improves its efficiency and effectiveness. Where there is no system, they create their own.

- They are accountable to a result
- They believe in themselves
- They have a fear of failure
- They have no escape route
- They make no excuses
- They don't bullshit themselves into thinking they are making it while faking it.
- They enroll, they do not sell
- They make it a game and they find the fun in the game
- They don't measure themselves by monetary means

At all times remember that to risk foolishly is to be a fool. You must think before you do. Action that is not well-thought-out can be misdirected at best and dangerous at worst. If you study the lessons of history, you will learn much about business. The following two stories provide an object lesson that distinguishes intelligent risk from irrational action.

RESISTANCE CHECKPOINT

Are you currently subject to a form of procrastination, perhaps avoidance of a project, the unwillingness to have a difficult conversation, or maybe you're thinking and making that half-baked commitment, "I'll start tomorrow"? The time to act is now. The shorter the distance between a deliberate thought and its decisive action, the greater the likelihood of success— the opposite is also true; choose to prosper by doing the former or succumb to the delay of the latter.

THINK BEFORE YOU DO

U.S. Army officer George Armstrong Custer sought individual glory, was intractable in his belief of his own superiority, and took a needless risk with his life and the lives of his men. In 1876, tensions with Native Americans came to a head at the Battle of Little Bighorn. Leading up to this, Custer had ignored information from his scouts—his eyes in the field—and instead signaled the trumpet charge and impetuously led 210 of his men into a valley of death. He lives on in legend, or infamy depending on your source of information, as an example of what ego careening out of control through careless risk can do.

The British Duke of Wellington, on the other hand, was patient. He understood risk. He also understood necessity. Napoleon, fresh from his exile on Elba, was seeking world dominion. Wellington knew the risk, but he also knew what he had to do. He was able to pick the terrain, assess the risks, and develop those allies who could contribute to the collective accomplishment. His thoughtful strategy allowed the British to defeat Napoleon at the Battle of Waterloo in 1815.

We have the choice to change our thinking. Thoughts are things; they take form. Choose to accept fear for what it is—an imagined experience that appears to be real. We've overcome fear in the past. The actions we take today will influence our future. Remember to think deliberately and act decisively.

ACTION STEPS:

→ Are you in position to win? Think of what it takes to win, formulate your strategy and then implement the tactics without hesitation, without waiver or doubt, and go for it.

→ Think of the steps or activities necessary to obtain something of value. Be very specific and clear with your goals. Now take the steps to limit your downside, know your risks, address them, and then move forward toward your goals. Don't waiver, once you commit, burn your boat and go! Fortune favors the bold.

→ Become your own determined advocate. Continue with your personal development, learn something new every day, think of how you can apply what you have learned and then take bold action to make it happen.

→ Think and do is a learned habit. It will take your instinctive feel, your rational thought, and your willpower to put those steps into action that create opportunities for your future. Keep this in mind and practice this habit every day—it extends beyond business into the realm of the personal. The more you do it, the easier it becomes, and the more effective you'll become in business and life.

SECRET #3

TIME WAITS FOR NO ONE

"Your time is limited, so don't waste it living someone else's life. Don't be trapped by dogma-which is living with the results of other people's thinking. Don't let the noise of others' opinions drown out your inner voice. And most important, have the courage to follow your heart and intuition."

— Steve Jobs

Time is our most precious commodity. Time is inelastic; none of us will get more—we each must make the best use of the seconds, minutes, and hours we have. In sales we waste massive amounts of time thinking (not doing) guessing, or becoming paralyzed by fear—this lesson on taking ownership of your time will reveal the most effective way to learn the difference between a person who uses you for a conversation, picks your brain for knowledge, and never intends to work with you, from one who is an interested prospective buyer. This secret will lessen the frustration of assumption. It will invoke the courage to question, and it will show you when to walk away from a bad position and a loss waiting to happen.

After a year of failed attempts, I was finally able to set up a meeting with a prospective client—a leader in his industry. All of the planning and the work began evaporating before my eyes, the result of poor time management on my part. I failed to anticipate the predictable traffic jams that are a part of our gridlocked existence in California. I'm screwed! I thought, stuck in stop-and-go traffic on the freeway. When I reached the company's gated compound, I was fifteen minutes late.

In sweaty dishevelment I made my way to the receptionist, where I was met with that look. I felt the shivers of frustration and fear extend from my spine. I fumbled for my business card and handed it to her, checking the backside to make sure it was clean, no phone numbers or scribbled notes. She made a perfunctory call to the requested party. She didn't glance up, her icy tone saying it all: "He will be out momentarily."

His steel company was prestigious and influential in the industry. I wanted to enroll this company in my portfolio. The prestige of association would build upon the foundation of my credibility. The door opened to the inner office. Those strategic plans were dashed when he began with a firm handshake and then a stern scolding.

"You're fifteen minutes late! It's a lack of respect for another person's time, and we don't get that time back. Consider the meeting cancelled and the lesson offered. Learn from this. It will be up to you to apply that lesson."

I was crestfallen—duly chastised for my lack of planning, foresight, and consideration. I wasted a year attempting to gain access to the man who had just laced me with a scolding. As I made my way to the car, I committed to a return. I burned with an intense need to prove myself. The validation was a crucible that I knew I had to overcome, own, and learn from in order to grow.

When you do the heavy lifting required to remove or eradicate the obstacles of ego, stubbornness, or fear, you will find the effort in the future less daunting from the benefit of the exercise in the present. If you don't address the tough issues in the present, you will always take a longer route, hoping to reach the destination in the future.

I spent the next year trying to claw my way back in. I began with a letter apologizing, and I continued to intermittently attempt to earn my way back in for even fifteen minutes of time. I was persistent and lucky—after a year of effort he gave me another opportunity. People quote Branch Rickey as saying, "Luck is the residue of design." Some of it is just luck, but design is a planned, prepared persistence and presence. When you plan and have the discipline to prepare, you can mitigate uncertainty, that part of fear that can make you doubt, hesitate, and then lose the advantage of initiative.

This individual had those qualities of character that could look beyond a misstep and offer a chance at redemption. I never asked him what it was that enabled my second chance. Perhaps he admired my persistence or maybe he just wanted to tell me in person to cease and desist. I was an hour early this time. Sitting across the desk from him with his stature and disciplined demeanor, I saw that look, that twinkle in his eye that promised more than a simple transaction if I could earn entry past the barrier that separated the many salespeople from the gate to his heart.

"Before we talk about business and what we do, let's talk about that which we can't get back. Do you know what we can't get back in life?"

As my face registered the canvas of blank expression, he saved me the embarrassment of struggling for the answer.

"We can't get back the words we say or write, the deeds we do, or the time we spend doing both," he said. "Time is inelastic. We will never get those seconds and minutes, hours, and days back. Don't squander time."

I listened as he continued, "It's always five minutes to midnight. We all need to remain aware of the value of time. Start focusing now on those things that matter. Do you know how important momentum is to a business? People create momentum. Momentum is that wave that you have to try like hell to start. When you're in a zone, you ride it, but if you stop it's very tough to regain. Your energy can create momentum if you effectively use your time to knock on the right doors, and in all cases, make sure you're on time!"

Leaning forward, his blue eyes reflecting instructive intent, he said, "We all only have twenty-four hours in a day—

what we choose to do with this allocation of time will impact our success and influence our destiny."

Destiny is forged in moments that often elude us in the present. In retrospect, in over twenty years of association, I can state without hesitation that the significance of this relationship is not amenable to monetary measurement. He became a lifelong client, but more importantly, a friend and mentor. His closing words to me endure as a living lesson to this day: "We can become devoted to an endless series of tasks that are designed to have no bearing on our intended outcome. It is simply an expansion of the hours we have to fill the day. Some engage in activity that bears no direct result on the preferred outcome. This is a waste of time, hours spent, watching the hands of the clock sweep by in a countdown to exit. It is a waste of time and a waste of life. Bill, make sure you do something for yourself every day. Break away from that damn phone of yours and take fifteen minutes or an hour to do something for you. You'll find the break rejuvenating. You need to make a date with yourself to spend some time doing something for yourself."

Driving home from the second appointment, I was straddling that chasm between exhilaration and the uncertainty of what the hell was happening. I burst through the door and didn't even bother to take my jacket off. I sat in front of the computer and began to formulate an email that would accomplish two things: first and foremost I would thank him for his time and consideration, and second I would recap the important points from our conversation:

Thank you for the time and consideration that you extended to me today with regard to the most important element that we can't get back in life.

The following is intended to serve as a summary from our meeting. I am forwarding them to your attention to maintain the accuracy and clarity of the message.

- *We create tasks to fill the void of time.*

- *We give ownership of our most precious commodity— time—to others on a whim or perhaps as a thoughtful decision. The key is to be judicious in how and with whom we spend time.*

- *When we decide to give time to another, we must do so with an understanding that we will never get the minutes, hours, or possibly, days or years back.*

Maintain a firmness of resolve and live with the pulse of passion. Don't spend life existing by wasting hours and days. Take time during the day to do something for you.

When we lose time in the web of resistance, we limit the experience that defines and cultivates a life in forward motion. We can lessen the impact of uncertainty by using our time to develop a plan. We must know that our plan may be met with an opposition that we have not anticipated. Uncertainty is a part of engagement. We can thrive in uncertainty, or we can succumb to the dragon of fear that would breathe this disabling toxin into our spirit.

We waste time when:

- *We perform activity just for the sake of activity, wearing out our minds, enervating our bodies as we traverse a path of circular motion that leads nowhere.*

- *We perform secondary activities and ignore our primary responsibilities.*

- *We choose the comfort of rote activity over that which requires competence, diligence, and more effort.*

- *We choose not to risk.*

- *We defer or put things off until later when acting now can make all the difference.*

- *Each of us is allotted the same amount of hours in a day: twenty-four. How we use the minutes and hours that comprise a day will contribute to our happiness.*

Be aware of those passing moments and minutes that you will never recoup. If knowledge carries an obligation to act, then use your time in the following ways:

- *Play it forward.*

- *Live congruent with your why, your purpose.*

- *Every day learn something new.*

- *Nothing happens without risk.*

I very much appreciate the philosophy and action orientation that defines and governs your leadership style.

Thank you again for your time and consideration. I truly appreciate and value your time and direction.

Sincerely,

Bill

I captured the collage of past experience, the memory of that first meeting, its significance, the difference it would make in my future, and thought about time. I agree that in life it is always "five minutes to midnight." Life is short regardless of span in terms of years, and it is subject to the laws of nature in its most tenuous state. Living life is a risk; there is no such thing as an existence that is hermetically sealed from the sands of time or the ravages of fate.

Are you moving toward your goal and destination, or are you engaged in the resistance of distraction?

Time flashes by—it seems like we're always running against the clock and into the wind. We run to the next appointment, fulfill the next commitment on our personal or corporate calendar, plan the next job, attend the next meeting, or set the next deadline. Choose to not waste time. Remember not to stay past midnight, personally or corporately. Each of us has a midnight. Every company has a midnight—be careful not to stay too long. Each of us is allotted the same amount of hours in a day, twenty-four. How we use the minutes and hours will largely determine our success and influence our happiness.

A KNIGHT'S ERRAND

Let's join King Arthur in his search for the Holy Grail. In the story of the grail, Arthur lay on his death bed, his heart representative of the barren wasteland he ruled. It was once a land that was vibrant, verdant, and infused with purpose. People were treated with respect and their lives flourished. When Arthur was betrayed by Lancelot and Guinevere, he sunk into the throes of a depression. Upon learning of the deceit, he banished both in anger from the kingdom—he felt betrayal and loss. His physical and mental capabilities waned from the regret of his outburst and the guilt of his reaction. He implored his quest knights to find the secret of the grail, hoping it would bring back life and restore the kingdom to its former vibrancy.

One knight returned. He relayed the following to Arthur, "As you go, so goes the land. You and the land are one." So it is with our thoughts and actions. When they are in alignment from the core of character, we are acting with an authenticity that is imbued with our values. We must be in alignment with who we are, what we say, and what we do. We must search for, face, and deal with our fears to become one. Our fears do not reside outside of us; they are within us.

This fable holds a distinct lesson for us. *People will feed from your energy.* They feel your energy from your emotional wake. Fear keeps us from making those calls, knocking on doors, and doing the unglamorous work that must be done before we can bask in the curtain call, bowing to achievement's internal applause. Some choose to busy themselves with needless activity and lose the minutes and hours of the day. We will never recoup those minutes and hours, the days, the weeks, or years. Opportunity does not lend itself to delay. Fear would have us lose our voice, search for conviction and purpose in the pages of a book or the rolling images of a YouTube clip.

Your self-belief and conviction will become compelling if you are compelled. Become compelling by believing in yourself and your purpose. Your voice will waiver and the flame will flicker in the sway of fear. Catch yourself, summon your courage, let your voice resonate from conviction and self-belief. People feel the authenticity in your voice; they see the flame of belief in your eyes—keep the flame burning, be compelled, and genuine.

THE PROCESS OF SALES COURTSHIP

First, seek a meeting in your prospect's office, and keep it short. Stay on point. The goal is to get to next—the next meeting, the next step in the process, or perhaps, next is a consummated sale. Find a reason to have another meeting. Build on the value premise and promise from your initial meeting. Follow-up after the meeting with an email thanking them for their time and consideration. In the email, outline the next mutually agreed upon step.

Play it forward by thinking and implementing the next step. Take the actions that move you closer to yes. Share information, entice them, be attractive, have an air of confidence, know your subject matter, believe in yourself. Exude confidence, but don't become careless or sloppy. If there is an interest or connection, it will pull you forward as it pulls them toward you.

Find a common interest. The conversation will either flow or not, just like when you are on a date. It's not easy to turn a bad date good, but it's easy to turn a good date bad. You can push your position and become aggressive, probably get slapped, or you can stay on the courtship trail and keep moving gently toward yes by having a personal bandwidth that directs activity from feel as much as thought.

I often ask questions about a person's background, where they went to school, where they grew up, how they earned their position. Sometimes, I'd ask, "Do you enjoy what you are doing and if so, why?" You may be surprised by the answers or non-answers to these questions, but they hold the key to what you do next, when you do it, and how you do it.

People know when you follow a sales formula or script. The process of qualifying is an opportunity to become familiar, learn and bond with a prospective client. The catalyst in the formula is you. Your personality and style, talent, perseverance, persistence, and timing must make the process come alive. Remember, people expect a certain approach, they expect to be sold and told. Dare to be you, enroll, engage and connect.

Stay away from personal problems and issues or beliefs that could be controversial or offensive. Establish those hooks of connection that tie you to the prospect from an emotional sphere. Once you adhere to their emotional side, you can weave and bond from those small hooks of connection. Fortify a stronger relationship from each and every interaction. Reserve each interaction without expectation of another. Fully immerse yourself in the present with the person. Learn how to earn future engagements. Earn the right by forging the bond that comes not from expectation and assumption, but from paying attention to your contribution to the relationship in the present.

In all cases, the prospective client is the one who determines if you have earned the right to proceed. At this point in the process, there may be a chemistry coalescing between you and the prospective client. When it is intense, its vapor is passion. Passion is felt, not relayed through words, it is an unspoken expression, a difference maker, it cannot be contrived or fabricated. Passion seeps from purpose and desire. Passion is the chemistry of the connection, that, when amplified, defines the emotional feel of possibility.

Remember to use the most powerful words in our language, "Please" and "Thank you". After each meeting, send a thank you to the prospective client for their time and consideration. It does not need to be pithy or a version of War and Peace, but it needs to be done with haste, it needs to be completed with accuracy and it needs to have substance.

Your approach must be one of confidence. Substance trumps style every time. The marriage of substance and style is a winning formula. Style can be the promise of potential, the form or the flow, but substance is the result, the actualized.

Emotion may provide an opening but logical progression is the bond that anchors belief to experience. Believe that you are the product. Learn as much as you can about the personality and purchasing disposition of your prospect. Remember to enroll, not sell. Keep in mind that enrollment involves small steps toward "Yes." Engage from the heart. Don't whine, plead, cry or beg, maintain integrity. People respect integrity, they console weakness but they don't want to partner with it. When the numbers part of your proposal comes into play, remember you might be attractive, you might be in spiritual alignment, and you might have effectively extended emotional care, but it has to make sense for the other person in terms of cost.

Use a velvet glove, iron fist approach. The velvet glove is the respectful approach of subtle but consistent pressure and the iron fist must hold your will and resolve to move your proposition and platform forward. This will require the skill of a surgeon, the feel of an orchestra leader and the heart of a warrior.

HOW DO WE DETERMINE OPPORTUNITY?

Sales involves a process that qualifies opportunity from conversation. You must ask the questions that gain clarity and direction. Without direction, you are simply guessing—

to guess wastes time, and time is money, time is energy, and wasted energy compounds fear. Those who guess move further away from cashing the check and closer to the deeper levels of resistance and fear.

Through the heart of this darkness is where the champion prevails. The champion may get wounded in the battle but will ultimately prevail and triumph by asking those questions that cut to the very heart of integrity. As a practice, I would always preface my statement with the following: "I get paid to ask the tough questions. I mean no disrespect, but I must try to gain clarity." I would ask questions about the process, about the existing relationship—questions that would inspire more questions—and I would listen carefully to the answers. I strove for as much clarity as one could obtain or receive from the dialogue.

THE ART OF QUALIFYING OPPORTUNITY TO ACHIEVE RESULT

The courage to qualify opportunity from occurrence is the difference between an order taker and a professional. Ask the tough questions in a professional manner. Listen to what is said, strive for clarity, and work toward a mutually agreed upon understanding of the message and its intent. Ask when in doubt—clarity and direction can streamline and tailor your efforts to best achieve the intended result.

Converting a suspect to prospect and prospect to client is a process. This process is also applicable to personal relationships. We must listen and apply what we learn. What we think is secondary to what the prospect does—what the prospect will do or not do is influenced by what they think and what we do. What we do emanates from what we think. We must shorten the distance between thought and action. Choose to make action directed and purposeful. Move forward through incremental wins. The goal is to get to the next step in the process, the next meeting, the next directed activity. Learn to think next and act now.

Life is emotional connection with people; it's personal engagement and it's feel. It's not the cold gloss of a brochure; it's not the worn-out rhetoric of a mission statement. It's the look into the eyes, the engagement from the heart, and the willingness to expend part of your soul, to bathe in the flush and feel of connection. Everything else is an awkward, fumbling premature position that probably won't generate the result you seek.

There are steps that breed familiarity and there are requisite imperatives that implore us to ask the questions and hear the answers as accurately as our subjective nature will allow. Gaining clarity of intent will offer a better understanding and a more focused direction that will better enable you to differentiate opportunity from exercise.

Ask those questions during the initial meeting which will offer the most expansive breadth of understanding and insight into a person's disposition and willingness to entertain your offer, thought or position. When a prospect is willing and able to entertain and value your offer, you will move closer to the goal of engagement. In sales, it is essential to have the fortitude and knowledge to ask the type of questions which generate an interest from the audience. Most of these questions should be open-ended. Just as in a romantic courtship process, the sweetest sounds a person can hear is the sound of their name and the sound of their voice.

A buyer wants to know you care about them before they care about what you know. They need to feel this—they feel it when your word and action is in alignment. All you can ever be is you—be authentic in your approach.

QUESTION

Question with genuine interest—be prepared and informed. Learn as much as you can about the company or the person you are meeting with before the actual meeting. Ask questions with purpose. Acquire the knowledge of the other person's position, agenda, and motive. This comes with time spent, observation made without assumption, and the experience of another's character through action. You are not an order taker, don't become one. The diner is closed. Learning about others is a process; it is a process that forges the steel of the relationship through time.

Don't show up and throw up! It's not about you, it's about them. Intelligence rules, instinct governs—think and do with head and gut. Ask questions and let the harmony of relationship ensue.

Think next; act now. Look in your mirror and ask, "What is going on in this process? What have I learned? Is there an opportunity, or am I using my confirmation bias to fool myself into thinking there is one?" Exhibit urgency from the parking lot. Send a thank-you for their time and use please where appropriate. This is a huge difference maker. It not only exhibits your urgency but it also reveals your manners. It will separate you from the masses who do not know how or care to do this. I earned a significant amount of business from this very basic behavior. Good manners are rare—they open the door to the heart.

When you recap the important points of the dialogue, five minutes after the meeting, with "please" and "thank you" and a follow-up action item to get to "next", you are manifesting the urgency that most only talk about.

LISTEN

Listening is a form of behavior that interprets sounds and applies meaning and linkage to the learned concepts that we term language. We can hear external noise; we can tune it out or pay attention to it in a rote sort of mindless distraction. Listening is a learned ability. Listening is formed from discipline, focus, and the enthusiastic willingness to learn.

The willingness to listen can help us understand. Listening activates ideas; it strengthens the platform of communication. Reality is founded upon the meaning ascribed from communication. Listening ties the message to the messenger. When our behavior is in alignment with our words, we establish a baseline of consistency and predictability. When we don't listen to the words, concepts, or phrases of another, we enter the realm of assumption and when we assume, we infer. When we infer and interpret without the benefit of clarification, we choose to hear, or fabricate, positive signs or words in the exchange.

We also tend to embellish or construe what we assume conveniently to be a positive or yes in the buying process. A prospect's verbiage may include, in its most promising form, a maybe. We can't cash checks from maybe. We don't earn the opportunity or seal the commitment unless we listen and apply what we learn for effect. Effect encourages positioning. We gain position and leverage when we listen and apply what we learn from the exchange.

Application of what we learn is a dynamic process. Sales is a dynamic activity. We must think and apply. We must learn and do. Those who sit and wait, then show up with a proposal or offer, may as well stay home on the couch watching cable television. The chances of getting on the next game show are about as good as sealing a commitment in the form of yes from a buyer. Small affirmative steps generated from thought, activate what we learn if we apply for effect.

- When we listen, we find the key in the phrase, the word in each paragraph.

- If we listen, we learn the way.

- We can then create a strategy and generate action that is consistent and in alignment with the other person's intent, message, and agenda.

We can learn how a person thinks through astute listening and observation; observation will yield patterns from activity that either support or belie the spoken or written word of another. In the dark fog of assumptive guess, a new Sherlock Holmes persona can emerge as the hero with awareness and a flashlight. Through this platform, we can employ our intuition and our elementary understanding of human nature. The nature and timing of our questions, the ability to listen, to separate what we want to hear from that which is said, and that which is said from that which is intended, is the difference between good, great, and the unemployment line. Deductive reasoning supported by questions, governed by intuition, bring clarity and light to the fog of darkness that is chance and guess. We must listen and ask. We must expand beyond hearing, as we listen to apply. How we apply what we learn, can and will make the difference in what we earn.

DO THE HEAVY LIFTING

Memorialize conversations in writing. Apply the rule of three. Tell the person what you are going to discuss. Discuss it and then ask for their understanding of what was discussed. Work until mutual agreement is found. Now, memorialize the understanding in writing. Take the extra step. Make the power of words work for you and know the importance of context and meaning in conversation.

THREATS AND OPPORTUNITIES

In life, as in business, we seek to forge opportunities and limit or eliminate threats. Think and deploy those allies and advocates who can assist you to maximize opportunity and limit threat. Maximize opportunity. Ask, "Where do I have the most potential to make a difference over the coming hours, days, weeks, or months? How can I position myself to do so?" Minimize threat. Ask, "Where am I most vulnerable and what limits or weaknesses do I have in thought and approach? Am I making assumptions or is what I think valid and consistent with the reality of the dialogue, connection, or relationship? What do I have to do to limit my downside and increase the chances for success?"

RESISTANCE CHECKPOINT

When you enter into dialogue with another, do you listen or speak first? Resist showing up and verbally throwing up; choose instead to listen.

IT'S TIME TO EITHER STAY ON THE DOCK OR GET ON THE BOAT

We are either on the boat of opportunity or on the dock of sanctuary. The boat of opportunity is always leaving. Let's examine the metaphor. The dock offers security of the known and a sanctuary for those unwilling to take the risks that are an inherent proposition in the bargain necessary to create opportunity. The boat of opportunity is always leaving. If we are indecisive, with one foot on the dock and another on the boat, we will soon end up in the water. The boat's destination (opportunity) is subject to the skill of the navigator (will and talent), the trade winds, currents, and weather patterns of the ocean (chance and adversity). We may become shipwrecked, we may be overtaken by pirates, we may crash into the rocks following the sirens' song of promise, or we may reach our tropical destination where we enjoy the fruits and nectar of a life that rewards our risk.

For those who choose to stay in the comfort of the known, on the dock, there is as much certainty as the uncertain prospects of life can offer. In a zone that is the comfort of the known, the landscape never changes. We can glimpse at the horizon and the constant procession of boats that are leaving the dock and only utter, "what if," "if only," or "not yet?" Or, we can, quite convincingly tell ourselves "it's not for us." When we know ourselves, our instincts, inclinations, and desires, limitations, and strengths, we can best make the decision to stay on the dock or get on the boat.

The boat may very well not be for all—it is for those that have that gnawing feeling in their gut, that compelling voice in their head, and that unsettling feeling that there just must be more. For these risk-takers, the boat symbolizes the passion of their purpose, and the willingness to attempt to live a life without regret by taking a chance and risking life over existence. The moral of the metaphor is found in the choice between boat and dock—choose one or the other but you cannot choose both. To attempt a compromise by straddling both, while not putting all of your heart and your soul into one or the other will leave you all wet, bobbing in the water, where sharks and box jellyfish await.

ACTION STEPS:

→   Listen and find the key phrase in each sentence you hear and read. There will be anchors, positional markers that will point the way, the direction. Find a way to listen, resist the temptation to talk over another, and make a way to apply what you learn.

→   Memorialize conversations in writing. Apply the rule of three. Tell the person what you are going to discuss. Discuss it and then ask for their understanding of what was discussed. Work until mutual agreement is found. Now, memorialize the agreement in writing.

→   Many people fail to follow-up on promises and their commitments ring hollow without execution. To be distinctive, you must follow through from request or promise to commitment, with a sense of urgency while consistently exhibiting the highest standards of professionalism.

SECRET #4

FIND A WAY OR MAKE A WAY

A melia Earhart had the courage to begin and the fortitude to continue. She was the first female aviator to fly solo across the Atlantic. On the side of her plane, in bold paint, was her mantra, "Always think with your stick forward." The statement references flight speed—you push the throttle forward to accelerate. To let up is to crash. You must be intelligently deliberate, but it is imperative that you move forward, always forward.

Earhart put herself in a position to achieve. She couldn't make a living as a pilot so she went into social work. Then, the offer came. She wasn't the first choice—someone had already backed out. She wouldn't get to fly the plane; there were two men that would accompany her. The men would get paid; she wouldn't. Uncertainty was part of the contract; death was an implied possibility. She accepted the offer. This was her foot in the door that was the start, the beginning, the building phase.

Within five years, Earhart became the first woman to fly nonstop across the Atlantic. She made the flight because she took the offer—even though it was a bottom-rung offer—and made things happen by moving forward.

IF IT IS TO BE, IT IS UP TO ME

Find a way or make a way. Mental toughness is a condition or state that differentiates average or good from great. Mental toughness is the ability to consistently perform toward the upper range of talent and skill regardless of competitive circumstance or personal distraction. The essential element of mental toughness is resiliency. Actualized, mental toughness enables one to find a way or make a way, create and forge opportunities, create and forge lifestyle, and create and forge legacy.

"Find a way or make a way" requires creativity and resilience to reach your goal. It demands the resolve to maintain the burning need to make a way forward when creativity requires a turbo boost from willpower. When you have exhausted the possibilities and intricate permutations of form, substance and style, you will need to draw upon your mental resilience and generate the toughness and resolve to make things happen in spite of the difficulty or obstacle. Many will quit, make an excuse and stop. Excuses are things you look for to rationalize your deficiencies. Those who move forward will lose the excuses and find or make their way to success.

TRYING TO TEACH A PIG TO SING

Make a choice to become an indispensable gift to your customer, coworker, and company. The bias of find a way or make a way is baked into your DNA. It will be with you when you join your employer or meet and marry your spouse. You will notice people either have a disposition to find a way to yes or check the box of no. Trying to turn a no bias into a yes bias reminds me of the lesson in the metaphor—if you try to teach a pig to sing, all you do is waste your time and annoy the pig.

Professional speaker and author Dean Minuto draws a distinction between a yes and no bias through the following story. As Minuto was embarking upon his whirlwind speaking adventures, he found himself at home in another airport. He had a new set of headphones for his iPad and needed something to open the seal of the package. He walked up to a rental car counter where a man and woman stood waiting to assist.

He asked, holding up the case, "Could you help me with this? Do you have a knife or something I could open this with?" The woman looked incredulous and replied, "This is an airport, no knives." The man stepped forward, took out his keys, and although in rough-hewn fashion, he managed to open the case. Guess which one had the yes bias and which one had the no bias?

In your life, there will be those who find a way to yes, and there will be those who follow an internal disposition and perhaps a corporate protocol to find no. This is one of the differences between those who don't and won't and those who can and do. You have a tendency toward a yes or no bias before you enter the workplace, it is a part of your DNA—you either are determined to find a way or make a way, or you default to no.

WILLPOWER

"Most people live—whether physically, intellectually, or morally—in a very restricted circle of their potential being. We all have reservoirs of life to draw upon of which we do not dream."

— William James

The freedom to make decisions, the fortitude to create choices and follow through from thought to action demands we call upon one of our most valuable resources—willpower. Strength of will is a resource that is finite—it can be depleted, but much like a muscle, it can also be strengthened and developed. Researchers have found that willpower is a better future predictor of success than IQ. While we are each born with varying amounts of willpower, science has proven that we can grow our willpower by using it, creating a plasticity that can expand our will beyond our genetic predisposition.

One of the differences that separate those who think and do from those who won't and don't is the ability to generate inspired action. Your habits will become your distinctive, signature style. Practice these habits until this becomes part of your nature. Facing fear is a learned habit. Taking the steps through fear is a habit. Overcoming adversity with resilience is a habit. Life will respond to the habits you own and direct.

Willpower is the game-changer in life. Think about it. At some point, everybody quits. Those with the greater willpower will endure, extend beyond, and reap the benefit of this power. Extend your result line every day—do something more, push yourself. Each time you extend today's level of effort beyond yesterday's, you assimilate the power of resilience. Resilience is conditioned—you can extend beyond your previous limits and the efforts that once seemed so difficult and foreign will now become the habit of the familiar. Push beyond habit, push to next, strive to gain and direct yourself to achieve the results that will make a difference in life and its subset, business.

Business is a sub-set of life. Life and business are not mutually exclusive, they are one in the same. There is life and the attending contributory requirements that forge and become lifestyle. Extraneous pursuits, things and distractions beyond the realization of meaningful goals and dreams must not encroach on your bigger purpose of attempting to live a life of meaning. Live your life the best way possible. As you make or find a way, there will be obstacles that impede your progress. Willpower is a force of resilience that can drive you through and beyond the obstacle.

Your physical energy must cash the checks that your mind writes. It responds to the voice that says, "I don't want to make that last call. I don't have to, I don't need to—I'll do it tomorrow." It responds with a resounding, "I must. I will. I am!" Willpower will help you break the barrier or extend beyond the threshold of pain and exhaustion. It will provide for new horizons—a baseline for new achievement. It will be the muscle that is used to move past a previous boundary and will give you the confidence to attack the next with the knowledge that you have the stamina to finish every job you start.

You can't do good business sitting on your rear. Willpower gets you off your chair. It's difficult to get up off the seat if you don't have the physical energy to push through a hard day. What you feed your mind provides inspiration and nourishment for the soul, what you feed your body gives you the fuel to make dreams reality.

THE MUSCLE OF HABIT

Willpower holds us to habit, and the resolve needed to face fear will call upon our strength of sustained determination. When we adopt the habit of taking those first steps and doing those things outside of our comfort zone, willpower can maintain our discipline of habit and the exposure to a new experience will become less painful each time we engage in it.

I have found that when I push myself in one area (for example, workouts), it is of tremendous benefit in other areas. Conversely, if I push myself in areas other than fitness, it draws upon the mental strength demanded to fire through an intense workout. Life is a trade-off, a game of balance. Transference of the physical and mental into a singular dynamic becomes a potent force for potential possibility—it extends the lesser power of two to the formidable power of one.

MOUNTAINS INTO MOLE HILLS

Willpower and habit are the weapons we need for immediate change. Long-term change begins with our influence in the subconscious realm. What I feed my subconscious becomes my conscious reality. When I feed and grow that finite muscle of willpower, I can drive through my fears by holding myself accountable to those habits that create a new way forward. I focus my attention and sharpen the clarity of my goals. When my goals are present and clear, my intention and attention is focused and free from distraction. If my attention is distracted, I wander down the alley of fear. Fear compounds from delay—if I wait, anxiety is heightened, the mole hill of doubt grows to a mountain of dread. Facing fear can raze the mountain to a mole hill. My imagination can create quite the impressive mountain range to overcome, but my disciplined will can reduce it to insignificance.

WILLPOWER: THE MARRIAGE OF FORTITUDE AND PERSEVERANCE

- Willpower is the inextricable marriage of fortitude and perseverance. Simultaneously performing several tasks that are unrelated, while bringing each to successful completion, can grow your willpower. You have to finish things off—stop and go without completion will deplete your willpower.

- Willpower transforms clarity of thought to directed action.

- Willpower turns challenges and obstacles into triumphs and successes. It is necessary for the completion of an objective, or the obtainment of a worthy goal.

- Willpower is the mental and physical embodiment of stamina and endurance—it can influence and determine the outcome of an engagement.

- Willpower is tenacity; the unrelenting exertion of mental and physical resilience.

- Willpower is the fuel of forward movement—it keeps you reaching and achieving.

- Willpower is the adhesive that makes you stick to your resolutions.

- Willpower is the bridge between a mere existence and a great life!

HOW TO BUILD THE WILL TO WIN

When we lift weights or engage in exercise that involves muscle resistance, the time involved under tension is what develops the strength and size of the muscle. Time under tension is continuous resistance—it is the time that your muscles are engaged in exercise. Just as the muscles can be developed, they can also be depleted by overwork. Growth from resistance training occurs during periods of rest. Willpower is much the same way. For instance, if we engage in a heavy workout and then, soon after, attempt to do some strenuous physical exercise, we won't have as much power as we did when our muscles were first under tension.

   When you extend your willpower on many small tasks or on a couple of large ones, for extended periods of time, you can deplete your mental fortitude. You need recovery periods where your will isn't expended. If, for instance, you extend your willpower during work, going all out to finish off a project that demands extreme will and then you take that client to dinner, beware of the dessert tray. You will have less resistance to the chocolate cake after expending willpower than you would if you didn't suffer from the depletion of this finite resource during the day. Willpower is finite, there is only so much of it, it is your power bar (not the candy bar), the invisible energy bar in life, and needs to be replenished. We can develop the muscle of will by extending ourselves a bit further every day. Try not to make difficult decisions in a state of willpower-depletion. You will be better suited to reserve those decisions until you are fresh with the reservoir of energy needed to make informed choices from challenging options.

- **Clearly define what you want.** Keep the big picture in mind and make the sacrifices necessary to learn what you want. Take small steps to realize the goal of the big picture.

- **Don't stay in a state of willpower depletion.** Focus your energy and know when to lay off and find the humor in a situation—stop pushing through things, learn to relax and let it go. Some positions are untenable or unwinnable. Attempting to surmount or overcome the unwinnable is like grinding gears in a car—loud noises, a lot of smoke and no forward motion. I know if I want to push myself at work, I have to lay off the extracurricular stuff in the gym.

- **Don't defeat yourself—manage your stress.** Pick your battles. Willpower originates in the prefrontal cortex of the brain. The prefrontal cortex can be damaged by stress, impairing the ability to help you exert your will. The prefrontal cortex needs to be fed—keep glucose levels steady by eating every two-and-a-half to three hours. Small meals and good carbohydrates replenish the supply needed for that calorie-sucking brain of yours. Here's a hint: position yourself to win by preparing your food a couple of days in advance. When you need a go-to, don't go to fast food. Prepare and have food available to keep your store of glucose steady.

- **Remain aware—learn how it all works together.** The brain prefers to preserve calories, choosing the rote or the safe, and life's imperative is to move forward. You move forward by owning the habits that willpower enforces. Feed the brain and rest it. Finish projects, but try not to extend that power-curve too far, too long or in too many places at the same time.

- **The ZZZ factor.** Sleep offers a big assist in the willpower-development department. It replenishes your energy and restores your brain for the challenges of the next day.

- **Exercise and eat properly.** This is an often overlooked but requisite criteria for success in life.

- **Solve, don't quit on problems.** There is a direct correlation between your stick-to-it resolve in the present and your future ability to execute and finish off a task, process, or project. Coming up short and quitting is a learned behavior just as finding the will to push through and finish is a developed one.

VISUALIZE TO REALIZE

Visualization is a concept we can read about, think about, and half-heartedly wonder about. But when we imbue ourselves with the clarity of vision and hold ourselves accountable to its vivid actualization, from the first step to the final step of realization, we awaken the dominant force of our subconscious. Our subconscious beliefs are more powerful than our conscious thoughts. When we activate, as Maxwell Maltz in Psychocybernetics terms our "auto-success mechanism," we command the subconscious to move toward that area we direct through the subconscious. When we find our definite purpose in life, fix it in our minds, and hold it with the determination of will and habit, our subconscious minds will influence the physical action of our bodies and move us toward the obtainment of our goals.

"True enjoyment comes from the activity of the mind and the exercise of the body; the two are ever united."
— Humboldt

For example, prior to a meeting with a prospective client, I would use internal dialogue to direct myself—I would be open to the experience, whatever it was, and not cling to a prejudice or a predisposed thought of negativity. I would just open myself to the experience. After the meeting, I would picture the process unfolding, in detail, all the way to yes. This process yielded immediate positive results. Visualization has become a habit, a way, an inculcated style. I would imagine the prospect calling and informing me we were the select choice. I envisaged him calling for assistance on issues—I played it forward in my mind, in living color, a year down the road. I imagined the person now as client and friend, writing unsolicited testimonials.

I did the same thing with my workouts. Before I would physically engage, I would mentally walk into the gym. I would picture the weight I was going to lift, imagine myself lifting it with ease for as many reps as I was going to do that day. Each time I channeled the visual to the execution of the actual, the weights felt lighter. If we try to rush or pull a heavy weight and we walk in cold, it's usually an exercise in joint and tendon damage.

When you're unprepared, the weights are cold and heavy and the resistance can be extreme. But I found that picturing the lift all the way through to its successful conclusion was much like meeting with a prospect that through a visualized, disciplined process of thought and activity was transformed into a client. When you let go and direct your subconscious from a suggestive, deeply ingrained belief system, it opens, enables, and creates a positive experience. Some things in life can't be explained; for the cynic, this is one of them. But those things in life that can't be explained are often the most powerful. I can't explain the energy of the universe. I find these things beyond my ability to enunciate and any such attempt would limit its ineffable beauty and do an injustice to its power.

HEAVY LIFTING

I would walk up to a weight, squeeze it hard, picture the lift, squeeze harder, think of the weight as Styrofoam, and make the lift. I would summon the energy, the intensity would release the adrenaline, and, without thought, I would complete the lift. Sometimes I was shocked by how light and easy the lift was. Our mind prefers to replay stories, both the good and bad experiences, and project them forward as future fact.

When we think of business as a game or as one of our preferred pastimes, it makes it much simpler to understand and navigate. We understand the joy of games or what we prefer to do for fun. When our bodies and minds are one, that union permits us to play loose and create a mental environment free of the need for perfection—a forum where we can have fun in the expression. We often try to separate business from our other pursuits, but it's all related. It's life.

When we label something as difficult, it will be. When we define a person with a defamatory expletive or limiting label, we tend to look for those characteristics which support our biased belief. It is our fear that seeks to marginalize others and maximize our version of self. We have an idea of the self and its importance in the universe; our ego supports our singular significance and doesn't like loss or change.

Loss and change shatter our illusions of self when we become attached to those things that can be taken from us. What we don't understand, we often limit or find a way to comprehend in our terms—that's fear doing its best and winning. It will take our heightened awareness to know when fear is forcing its limits upon us. Summon the willpower, find courage of heart, and open yourself to possibilities beyond the fearful limits of ego. Here's the great news: we can do all these things. This isn't motivational drivel, we can do this. We can become aware of our bandwidth, our emotional current; we can grow willpower; we can take small steps from habit; we can move through fear, feel better for the process and enjoy the result.

Visualize what you want with clarity, resolve to get it, and find a way or make a way to obtain it. What is keeping you from happiness, excitement, adventure—from fulfilling a destiny that only you can forge? Choosing life over existence is worth the sacrifice. At times it will be a struggle. Find the allies and advocates in your life that can help you continue on your quest. Things will go wrong; it is always darkest before the light. When you accept fear as an inevitable fact of life and reject it as a source of preordained powerlessness, there is little that can hold you back. When you have the resolve and are compelled to move forward, the pull from purpose will trump the pain, disorientation and dissonance of fear.

RESISTANCE CHECKPOINT

Are you willing to adopt the habits and take the small, disciplined steps to make the changes you need to face and move forward through fear?

TO DEVELOP THE MUSCLE, WE HAVE TO FEED THE MUSCLE

How do we grow willpower? By using it. Each time we extend ourselves just a little bit further, we can expand our willpower. The body is the temple that houses our mind, the center of our reality. What we feed both is what we will become and project to the external. Nutrition is paramount—we have to feed the prefrontal cortex, the locus of our willpower. It responds to sugar, but no, don't drink a Coke. You can get nutrition from complex carbs as well. A complex carb or a protein every two-and-a-half hours will feed the brain and create the best energy for willpower use. The term ego depletion refers to the limits of self-control or willpower. We have a limited pool of mental resources. When the energy for mental activity is low, self-control is typically impaired, and we would be considered to be in a state of ego depletion. When we are in this state, we have less control over habit and are more inclined to make decisions that are constricted or impaired by this state. It may be wise to eat something and let your glucose levels rise, before you make that tough decision or start to burn those calories from critical thinking.

We all have a finite level of willpower. For example, let's stay in the gym. When I'm in a vicious business cycle, running full out, it doesn't behoove me to do a maniac workout and deplete my willpower in the morning. If I want to have a productive day at work, and burn my willpower for business purposes, I have to reserve the workouts for night. I don't have the same willpower at night as I do in the morning if I burn through work, but life is a trade-off. You can strive for Mr. or Ms. Olympia, or summon the singular resolve to drive forward and create the next opportunity.

Can you do it all? In all walks of life, there are outliers and black swans, those people with the capacity to expand their will— those who replenish and refocus from the furnace of their purpose. They're out there. Do you have it within you to become one of them? I learned a long while ago that is very difficult to maximize two variables simultaneously. The personal wisdom of experience is a constant reminder of my limits, and it keeps me in check when I attempt to extend willpower in too many areas simultaneously.

I have developed the ability to resist the temptation of some things sometimes, but not all things at all times. The more clear my goal and the deeper my emotional connection to its achievement, the lesser the pull of temptation. The more compelling need will trump the convenience of short-term joy, comfort, or distraction. I know the sweetness of chocolate cake will taste great for two-and-a-half seconds, but it will smear my abs in its decadence and take twenty-five minutes of intense workout to even begin to work it off. Now, I do have my days when I let it go and have cheat meals—sometimes they last all day. Cake, pizza, ice cream, I just go for it. It relieves the mind of tension, replenishes the will and fires up my metabolic furnace. I find that by letting go, my willpower bounces back the next day. Refreshed and refueled, I am ready to engage, enroll and continue on the quest to improve my personal and business platform. Success is crafted from the small steps that enable the quantum leaps forward. This is the marriage of visualization and actualization at its highest form.

ACTION STEPS

→ Move forward—become compelled to do that which others won't or fear they can't. This is often what it takes to win the moment, the minute, the hour, the day.

→ Develop your willpower. Willpower can grow stronger, just as the muscles of the body do when they are used regularly and pushed beyond the zone of comfort. This is where the duality of mind and body growth occurs.

→ Feed your brain. Nutrition is paramount. Complex carbs and lean protein every 2.5 hours will nourish the brain and create the best energy for willpower deployment. Fun fact: the brain runs off sugar; the heart thrives from good fats. (Author's Hint: lean protein, eggs, poultry, grass-fed beef, small portion sizes every 2.5-3 hours, regulate the blood sugar, and nourish the prefrontal cortex, the epicenter of our will; sweet potato, not yam, there's a difference—for good carbs; and fish, macadamia nut, olive or coconut oils for good fats.)

→ Know what you want with clarity—think long-term; act now. Be willing to pay the price, but first learn the cost of the obligation. When we are willing to make the payment in sacrifice and effort, we are ready to face fear.

→ Learn what you can and cannot control. Adjust your mindset accordingly. By doing so, you will alleviate the needless stress that evaporates willpower.

THE RULE OF 33-1/3 PERCENT

A young salesman, straight out of college, entered my office one day, flush with frustration. His exasperation emanated from a lack of response and the unwillingness of some to listen to his pitch. I heard the struggle in his voice and noticed the uncertainty in his eyes. There was a concern in the tone of his question and an underlying doubt in its content. He asked me to help him convince people to talk to him. He was looking for magic, a surefire approach. I imagined his internal mirror reflecting lower self-esteem or self-worth each time people refused to listen to him. I decided I would help him understand the impersonal numbers game of business. We must learn and then adopt a mindset that distinguishes between the personal and impersonal aspects of business. Unless there is a connection with people that extends beyond the numbers and product, business is more of a transaction than consultative partnership. Where there is a connection with people that extends beyond the numbers and product, there is emotional engagement. Emotional engagement is, by definition, very personal. He took a seat and I shared my "Rule of 33-1/3 Percent" with him.

33-1/3 percent is a mindset, not a strict formula based on science. The 33-1/3 percent is a part of "Activity Rules Success," a numbers game. And to win the game of numbers, you must understand that rejection is not personal; it's part of the game of business. When you own this rule and accept its premise, you'll limit the sting of rejection and begin to understand it's just a numbers game.

In my rough formula, 33-1/3 percent of people are not going to buy you or your product for their reasons. Those reasons may have less to do with you and more to do with the established beliefs that control their thinking. You can attempt to convince, cajole, or buy the loyalty and purse of the unwilling. But the unwilling will find alternate avenues to a similar destination that will not include you or your proposal. They are resistant to the message, the messenger, or both. They resist any change that is inconsistent with their belief system (maybe they purchase your product from a family member, a friend, or there are forms of nefarious politics involved—things outside of your control, things you don't and perhaps won't know).

Opportunity resides as a 66-2/3 percent proposition. If 33-1/3 percent of people don't buy you or your product for reasons stated above, that leaves 66-2/3 percent ripe and ready for your approach. They are willing to believe. You can enlist them to your platform if you can earn the right to their hearts. Disappointment follows rejection and can make you withdraw from the game. What is needed to enroll is enthusiastic engagement—stay mentally tough. There is a rich environment for your success, and it consists of 66-2/3 percent of the population. Remember, the rule is a mental formula that can keep you from the disappointment and wasted effort that comes from a need to try to convince everyone you talk with to join your position or buy your proposition. The numbers game of more opportunities multiplied by the ability to qualify an occurrence from an opportunity will make a difference in the success of your efforts. "Activity Rules Success," the law of sales and life is a numbers game. The more we do, the more we enroll, the more action we take from thought, the greater the likelihood of success in our life, and I think the opposite is also true.

People buy from people they like. Is this an all-inclusive, all-encompassing law? No. Like any rule, there are exceptions that prove the fallibility of the rule. I will lean on the labors of those who conduct studies of human nature to support my thesis. I would suggest you turn to Robert Cialdini's book *Influence: The Psychology of Persuasion* to validate my statements.

INSIDE THE NUMBERS

When we have a bigger base of suspects to qualify to prospects, fear and desperation are ushered out of the room. Be selective and intelligent in your approach. Remember, *"Activity Rules Success."* Confidence ensues when a salesperson conveys authentic, passionate self-belief and takes ownership of the sales process. We will gain more when we are not desperate or unable to listen to what is being relayed. Listen and apply what you hear. Stop believing that an opportunity exists when, in fact, it may not. Practice *Activity Rules Success* and live the application of *Think and Do!*

RESISTANCE CHECKPOINT

People smell fear and desperation. They feel confidence from the flush of proven success. Avoid setting yourself up to lose. Position yourself to win. Select those opportunities where you have a chance to win and avoid those engagements that will entangle you in loss, fear, and frustration.

Experience is the best teacher—it is a tutor that will prevent the waste of time that is a product of selective hearing instead of active listening. There's a difference between a conversation and a qualified opportunity. When you learn to walk away from meetings that are mere conversation, not true opportunity, you'll preserve time and mental energy for other opportunities that you can bring to successful fruition.

In sales, head, heart, feeling, and a good volume in the pipeline will do much to eliminate desperation. When we are desperate, we are unattractive. Confidence, not desperation, is attractive. If we are attractive, we may be more likable. If we are more likable, we are more able to influence those like us who have an appreciation for and a connection to us.

PEOPLE CHANGE FOR THEIR OWN REASONS

We cannot change people, but we can influence them if they are willing to listen. People change themselves when they feel the need and are compelled to author the change. They change in their way—for their ideals, dreams, desires, and demands. They will change, adopt, and adapt in their way, through their form of means and methods, with or without our assistance.

ACTION STEPS:

→   Understand that rejection is often not personal. Choose not to make one rejection a point of resistance that detracts or delays your pursuit of future goals.

→   33-1/3 percent of people are not going to buy you or your product for their reasons. Know that you may never get the actual motive behind a reason or decision. Learn to live with the fact of this reality. Activity rules success—it's the law of survival in the business jungle.

→   Stay mentally tough. Success is not final, failure is not fatal.

SECRET #6

WALK AWAY POWER

I learned to pull back to attract. You make yourself much more desirable when you're not desperate. People smell three things on you: desperation, fear, and greed. No amount of perfume or cologne will cover any of them up. In any negotiation, he or she who cares the least controls the most—my acronym is WAP, Walk Away Power. You start making money when you stop focusing on every dollar, when your compelling reason is beyond the material, when you maintain your self-respect, realize your value, remain humble, persistent, and always in forward motion.

Take caution not to negotiate against yourself. This happens many times in life, when we devalue our proposal, proposition or person. Since birth, you have been negotiating; bargaining for authority, information, opportunity, time, and affection. Develop negotiation skills that bring more of what you want and less of what you do not. Broaden the scope of your negotiations. Take into account all known elements of an issue. Piece together wins for the other side. Know your non-negotiables. There is a point where you walk away, perhaps not because you care the least, but because you are unable or unwilling to relinquish the financial or emotional concession the other party demands. You lose all future bargaining strength if you negotiate away your values, character, or self-respect.

Never assume to know what the other party wants. Commit first to learn about the person you are negotiating with and then learn about the prospective business deal or life event. Understand that people are unique and may reluctantly reveal agenda and motive, but underneath the cape of nondisclosure, the true object of desire resides. You must be able to remove the cloak to reveal the answer.

Know that prior to and during negotiations we must establish the rules of engagement and develop the criteria to be discussed. We are best served when we can gather information about the other side: personality, disposition, business acumen, level of street smarts, and previous record of negotiation. We must reach agreement from a middle or common ground. To reach common ground we may have to give away the stuff that does not really matter. Make it a point to give it up slowly.

Dropping price is often not the most effective method of negotiation, but a form of capitulation. If one party dictates price, the other party can dictate terms. The obverse is also true. Remind yourself that negotiation is a process. If people are still standing in front of you, literally or metaphorically, they are still negotiating.

Be aware that if you extract or demand unfair terms or conditions, you may achieve a pyrrhic victory. A pyrrhic victory is a victory in name only, at a very high cost. It's when the cost of the win is really tantamount to a defeat. If people feel they are unfairly treated, they will find a way to extract that pound of revenge from you in some form with or without your consent. This is why it is important to have both parties, whenever possible, walk away feeling good about the process and, most important, the result.

Do not bargain away your soul. You have to feel good about the outcome of the negotiation or the unsettling feeling will remain with you and taint future forms of negotiation with the residue of the past.

Know the strength and weakness of your position. Who has the most leverage? You or the other side? Think about the acronym WAP. How much you want or care about what they have will dictate what you are willing to give up to obtain it. Exert caution to not give away your personal value or power for money. Usually the person who holds the purse is the one who controls the negotiation. If the person attempting to earn some of that purse is willing to abrogate their personal standards and self-respect, weakness of character is now on exhibit. Proceed according to your compass of integrity and your definition of the rules of business. It takes discipline and will, understanding and respect for the self to not cave for the money.

Negotiation is a trade-off. In true negotiation, you do not gain something without giving something up. The value is contingent upon the worth you or the other party assigns to it. Negotiation is fluid. It involves discussion. It is best served without personal attack. Stay on point. Focus on issues, problems, rewards, and results, not personality. Personality is a byproduct of becoming acquainted with the person with whom you are negotiating.

You may have to negotiate with yourself to maintain a level of self-esteem and confidence in the face of adversity and frustration. Adversity and frustration emanate from the unwillingness to attempt or the failure to achieve. It is also an outgrowth of the disappointment that stems from unmet expectations. The nature of your self-talk is essential to the development of self-esteem and confidence. Self-esteem and confidence are the externalized expression of your persona. People feel the energy of your presence and the authenticity of your confidence or they feel the vacuum of your withdrawal and the limits of your self-belief.

RESISTANCE CHECKPOINT

As you negotiate in life, do you maintain your self-respect, or do you sacrifice it on the altar of temporary success? Don't bargain away your self-respect. Only you can give it away—know that once you do you can never get it back.

Apply the law of trade-off. What are you willing to give up in order to get what you want? Adversity, frustration, disappointment, and loss make us question our self-worth, confidence, and ability. When we look into the abyss and uncertainty or fear stare back, we must summon the courage and prevail upon our knowledge of self to overcome its debilitating illusion. Most fear is just that—an illusion of something imagined in the future. We all get hit, shaken, and sometimes stirred. It's what we do when we dust ourselves off and get up that makes the difference and shortens the gap between possibility and result.

ACTION STEPS:

→ Take caution not to negotiate against yourself. It takes restraint in those moments of silence, the minutes, hours or days when you are not actively engaged with the other party in the negotiation. Tempting as it may be, lowering your price, enhancing the terms, or otherwise trying to sweeten the deal without impetus from the other party will weaken your bargaining position.

→ Know your non-negotiables. There is a point where you walk away, perhaps not because you care the least, but because you are unable or unwilling to relinquish the financial or emotional concession the other party demands.

➜ Never assume to know what the other party wants. Commit first to learn about the person you are negotiating with and then learn about the prospective business deal or life event.

➜ Reach agreement from a middle or common ground. To reach the common ground, you may have to give away the stuff that does not really matter. Make it a point to give it up slowly.

SECRET #7

YOU CAN'T DO GOOD BUSINESS SITTING ON YOUR ASS

T he greatest salesperson I ever met was my Uncle Joe. He was the top salesperson at Union Carbide and his office was palatial. Not that he would know, because he never spent time in his office. To me, his office was his car, the front seat of a Cadillac. He pressed a lot of flesh and spent all of his time in front of customers. My Uncle Joe wore Italian suits that were immaculate and bold ties. His tie clip bore the acronym: YCDGBSOYA. I remember asking him about that tie clip when I was a teenager. I was sitting on the couch on a Sunday afternoon watching a football game and he, befitting his nature, was in work mode.

"Uncle Joe, what do the letters on your tie clip mean?" I asked.

He said, "Billy, you can't do good business sitting on your ass!" He was animated, pointing his finger at the tie clip and then me. With that, he was out the door on the way to lunch with a client. Life needs more people who are willing to launch out of their comfortable chairs and follow this example.

Here are some lessons I learned from my uncle:

- You separate yourself from the field when you get in front of people and become the human form of your brand.

- Remove your fingers from the keyboard and make the personal dynamic the variable that works in your favor.

- Make something happen by knocking on doors and meeting with people.

- The personal touch will establish and strengthen connection. Email, text, and phone are an impersonal form of remote control, a necessary convenience.

- Where possible, strive to get out and have a face-to-face conversation.

- Whether you serve internal or external clients, you need to engage with people. Too often we send internal emails to a person three doors down or avoid their calls or physical presence.

ABE: ALWAYS BE ENROLLING!

Enrollment is a process, it is like running for office and never getting elected. You must always shake hands, win hearts, and gain the vote of confidence from another. Consider this:

- When is the last time you influenced someone?

- When is the last time you sold someone something?

- Do you like to be sold; do you like to be told? Or, do you like to be enrolled?

- How did you influence them? What did you say? How did you say it?

- Did you do it over the phone, over email, or in person?

Now is time to get out; launch from your office; get out of the car; get on the street; meet with your clients and prospects, face-to-face, shoe leather on pavement, knuckles on doors. There will be an endorphin release and those that push themselves will know the feeling I'm referencing. It's a runner's high; it comes from physical activity. When you feel this form of release with an attending form of good tired, you'll feel like you've accomplished something for the day. Don't let your backside become a cushion; don't be a slug. Get out there with enthusiasm and energy. Show people you want it. You show people you want it when you show up present, professional, and polished. Many opportunities are made available for people who just show up. It's the law of attrition or addition by subtraction. Show up with resolve of purpose and clarity of message. Hustle creates opportunity. Hustle is shoe leather on pavement. It's pressing flesh. It's the resilience to make the extra call, and it's the extra effort to remain visible in the sight lines of your customer or those significant others in your life.

GAINING THE EDGE

I love the art of the deal. I embrace the sales process as enrollment, winning hearts, and serving as a determined advocate for the business welfare of others. Sales is the tip of the sword, it is the edge. A sale extends beyond transaction and becomes consultative when the seller's process, program, and product protects the buyer's people, product, and profit. Sales are the edge to a company's growth—it doesn't exist by job definition; it is the duty and responsibility of everyone in the company.

What does the edge look like and how do you gain the edge?

- You gain the edge when you lose excuses, reasons, and conditions for failure. Success is the product of personal accountability, perseverance, and the applied lessons of failure.

- The edge accepts failure as a part of success.

- You gain the edge when you learn the cost of success and embrace the sacrifice necessary to realize it.

- You gain the edge when creativity becomes action—where you think and do with purpose and conviction.

- The edge is knowing when to pull back, push away, or walk away from a bad position.

- The edge is distinctive because it dares to be different, open, transparent, and vulnerable. Connecting to the heart of others is vulnerable, but people buy from emotion first—connecting to the heart is where true engagement occurs.

- The edge isn't trying to be perfect or superhuman—it's the commitment to be prepared, authentic, and transparent.

- The edge prepares to compete and competes to win.

- The edge is always moving forward—forward wins the moment, delay will lose the day, month, quarter, year, and perhaps cost you your career.

- You get the edge when you follow the process that converts a suspect to a prospect and prospect to client.

- The edge asks, "How would I compete with myself?"—and then addresses the assumed deficiencies in approach or position, product, or service.

- You gain the edge when you learn that perfect is the enemy of good.

- You gain the edge when you break away from the fear of trying to make the perfect choice. Work to create the conditions that enable a best possible choice. The key is to make a choice. Think next, act now by making a choice.

THE CHEMICALS OF CONNECTION

Fears stack up and delay, creating and compounding the painful possibility of failure. Move your value proposition forward, always forward, by living the spirit of YCDGBSOYA. Most will be playing catch-up to your lead. Don't wait for the call—make the call. Get out and press flesh, because others won't—they are comfortable in the confines of their office or environment. Stretch, think, do— there is a power in its simplicity, a challenge in its execution, and a difference in its result. Walk down the hall, meet with your co-workers, have a discussion, not an email exchange.

"On the field of the Self stand a knight and a dragon. You are the knight. Resistance is the dragon."

— Steven Pressfield

Oxytocin and serotonin are the chemicals of connection—they are released from pressing flesh. Pressing flesh to a keyboard often releases a message of ambiguity and encroaches upon time that could be spent meeting people and developing relationships.

GENERATING, MAXIMIZING, AND MAINTAINING MOMENTUM

Stay active in mind and body; do that which follows thought with vitality, purpose, and vibrancy! Momentum builds from the previous day, week, and month. It takes a tremendous amount of effort to achieve true momentum and relatively little inactivity to lose it. Start your day with the intent to maximize opportunities in a diminishing time frame. Every day opens a new window of time—use your time by learning the difference between what is important and what is redundant or secondary to the primary objective.

Think with audacity. Think with "What if?" as your primary question. Forget the "How?"—that's execution; for now it's all about concentrating on creativity. Think of yourself becoming free from chains or constraints that would limit anything but the possibilities of "What if?" Create a state, a zone of flow. Just let yourself go and answer the question, "What would happen if I do this?" Now do it.

Think the night before about the activity and the objectives or accomplishments you will achieve the next day. Visualize the achievements in detail. Set goals in sequential order of importance and get them off your list—execute! Visualize moving through an event in your mind. It will lessen the fear of unknown future performance.

Understand that the nature of life demands flexibility as floating objects come across your field of vision in the form of last-minute requests, unexpected events, and other interruptions in your daily productive routine. Embrace the fact that there is no such thing as routine. Prioritize your work. Use time to do what matters now. Some people think in linear form. Life is not linear. People are not linear. We can anticipate and expect an effect from some causes, but not always. Linear thinkers become frustrated and often have no Plan B when their expectation is met by the unpredictable. Expect the unexpected—you will not often be disappointed. Think worst case, anticipate, and be prepared—a recipe for taking on the unpredictable in life.

Victory is a choice involving the maximization of time and the achievement of daily incremental wins. Keep your momentum flowing forward by managing your time instead of allowing time to manage you. Plan and commit. Prioritize and deliver. Get things done. Commit to yourself that every day you will find a way to win some part of the game of business. It may be solving a problem for your client, obtaining a new appointment, knocking on a door— anything that moves you closer to your goal maintains momentum. Find a way to incrementally achieve or win the day over the obstacles that impede total victory. The small wins will add up to a big victory if you apply this theory to practice. Victory is cashing the check, buying the house, or donating to the charity of your choice. Victory has options. It provides lifestyle.

We will never recoup time wasted, and time wasted is anything that detracts us from our goal of succeeding in business.

We each have an internal feedback mechanism. We know when we are putting forth our best efforts and when we are not. The feeling is sometimes muffled by delusion or an unwillingness to look introspectively with honest appraisal, but deep down we all have that gnawing feeling when we waste time. Do not be deterred by setbacks or sidetracks; keep moving forward to achieve incremental wins every day.

WE WILL GET HIT, WE WILL GET KNOCKED DOWN

When the proverbial bullets or punches fly, we will figure out what to do. We will be resourceful. Some things cannot be trained; they must be assimilated from experience. There is a military axiom that Mike Tyson, the boxer, not the cartoon series star, used early in his career; *"Everyone has a plan 'til they get punched in the mouth."* The best, most thought-out systems and approaches, all the hours and days and months of training can prepare you for some, but not all, of what you will experience in the arena of business. Once that door closes behind you in a conference room or you meet with the person in the corner office, it is game on, and the game always changes.

People don't forge relationships with systems. People buy from people, from emotion and support their emotional decision with logic. While the door may be open through emotion, it remains open when logic enters and supports emotion.

YOU HAVE TO DO THE WORK

Larry Bird had a surplus of talent but he rolled out of bed every morning and stayed late in a desolate gym every night shooting more jump shots than any of his teammates. Michael Jordan worked on his moves and expanded his repertoire of shots long after and hours earlier than anyone else. Tom Brady continues to refine and elevate his position as an elite quarterback after four Super Bowl titles. This last line was particularly hard to write. Pittsburgh Steeler black and gold is inculcated into my emotional imprint—it's a rite of passage in Western Pennsylvania. One of the themes of this book is to strive for personal freedom, to gain perspective and distance from the emotional waves of the external. Although my rational thought can provide logical alternatives and an understanding of the nature of sport, my emotional state often depends on the outcome of the previous week's Steelers game.

Star outfielder Andrew McCutchen of the Pittsburgh Pirates has the following to say about what separates good from great: "I'm not big on politics. I'm more interested in just changing the way people look at things and helping others. Even if it's just other baseball players. A lot of guys like to ask, 'How do you do it?' I think what separates the good from the great is their minds. You've got to have something up there that just triggers you—something that shoots you off and helps you think in a certain way. You look at all the great players in the past, and they're going to tell you something about the game that makes you think; I never looked at it that way. Because it's just how they are. That's just the way the greats think. Someday I would like to be one of them."

"I have never known a man who died from overwork, but many who died from doubt."
— Dr. Charles Mayo, Co-Founder of the Mayo Clinic

Willingness and effort don't cash the check of result. I paid an expensive lesson to learn that no matter how much a person purports to want something, what differentiates want from result is in the work.

As I began to write, I reflected back on lessons learned in business and life. In the pages of this book, I have made every attempt to convey my experience, positive and negative, in the hopes that the reader will find a shorter distance and less pain in the realization of corporate and personal gain.

At times, I think ego blurred my vision of reality and I connected the profile of the new performer with that of past performers who met, eclipsed and then established an extremely high bar of performance expectations. I thought our system could improve performance simply because it existed. The system is nothing but an idea or concept without the people who give it life and breathe passion, performance and result into it daily. Consistent effort is something that is individualistic; it comes from an emotional place, from the shadows, it is a vision of the future and it is something that you cannot give, inspire or alter in a person.

I paid in hard costs and emotional pain. No matter how much desire or willingness to work a person exhibits, they must have a certain amount of innate ability to flourish.

WE CAN'T DRESS IT IN LINGERIE AND CALL IT SEXY

We live in a world of instant gratification and entitlement. A world that screams, "Move me ahead tomorrow and pay me today for ten years' worth of future earnings. I'll take them in bearer bonds." There is a fundamental law that exists in life and business: There is no escaping the dirty work. You can't dress it in lingerie and call it sexy. You can mess with it a bit and call it a game, but at the end of the day it's still a four-letter word: work. You have to do the hard work—the unglamorous stuff that gets your nails dirty and maybe even breaks a few.

Be willing to get your hands soiled by doing the dirty work—the basic work and fundamentals that provide the underpinning for the initial survival of the endeavor. When I was a child, my father often took me fishing, a hobby that with patience and skill can actually produce food. I wasn't a skilled angler, but I did the requisite work of collecting bait. Stealth, patience, and nimble fingers are the skills required to find and pull an earthworm from a garden or yard. I had the exercise mastered. I have captured hundreds of these nocturnal crawlers. Nightcrawlers or earthworms will come out of their holes at night after a summer rain floods their homes. They take the opportunity above ground to mate, find food, and release their excrement. Fish find these crawlers a delicacy so it is worth the extra effort to secure them. Maybe it was a metaphor for the future—searching in the dark, the wet, slimy mud—the only source of navigation, a small flashlight. It was the dirty work, the willingness to get down, crawl through the mud, and know that the purpose of the exercise would yield a form of pleasure in the future.

We had to get our nails dirty to collect bait the organic way. We were in miserable conditions, hunched over in search of that which crawls out of holes in the muddy ground. I use this analogy in business because allocating the time and effort to seek, find, think, and master those things that make a difference is going to be worth it. You will know the things to focus on because your fear will direct you to them. You fear most what you need and want at the most urgent and extreme level of internal connection. Feel the fire, go past the resistance, through the fear, and make it happen. No one can do it for you. You can't do someone else's push-ups for them; if they want to look good at the beach, they have to hit the floor and do their own.

In business there are no shortcuts to success—especially if the shortcut violates professional conduct. There are always faster, more efficient, more effective ways of doing things, but these means and methods can never come at the cost of our personal and professional standards.

PURPOSE ENSUES FROM THE WORK

You have to do the work. Sometimes the more diligently you search for something, the further removed it is from your grasp. Searching for purpose or conviction will blind you to its embrace. Experience and feel it—it can't be contrived or fabricated. When you actively search for purpose, you are in the dark without a flashlight. When you live true to your internal voice and pursue life in the spirit of authentic direction, you become the embodiment of purpose, passion, and conviction. When you become immersed in the work, there will be the feel of something that is beyond the job description, something that attaches to purpose. Purpose will find you when you become immersed in the work.

SMALL STEPS FORWARD CREATE MOMENTUM

The principle of inertia, described by Isaac Newton in his first law of motion, is, "An object not subject to any net external force moves at a constant velocity. Thus, an object will continue moving at its current velocity until some force causes its speed or direction to change." For example, if we slide a book across the floor, it would keep moving indefinitely unless it faces resistance. If the book does not hit an object or some form of resistance, it will be stopped by the force of friction. The friction people encounter is resistance from fear. Momentum is generated from the first step.

It takes courage to take that step, but you will take it and you will move through the obstacle of fear. Forward motion is not an option—it is a requisite to survival. Start taking those small steps forward and you will meet the guardian of sacrifice. You will learn to sacrifice your illusion of security, extend your circle of comfort, and intelligently risk taking those incremental steps that will make the tangible and intangible difference in your life.

Be aware that a life, regardless of span of years, is short. Be aware of the impact that choices make in the quality of our years. Every day we make a choice to get out of bed or stay in the cocoon of comfort under those warm sheets. Once we decide to get out of bed and our feet hit the floor, we make another decision. The next decision is to move off the bed and take the first steps of the day.

FIRST YOU HAVE TO GET OUT OF BED

Here's one from the annals of legend, a classic that burns an indelible mental image. Isaac Newton, shackled by the creation and construction of the thoughts he formulated, remained sitting on his bed with his feet on the floor, unable to move for hours. Now that's deep thought. He also used his body as a host for his various experiments. He once stuck a sewing awl, that long, dull needle, into his orbital socket to see what it would do. Fortunately, he wasn't irreparably harmed by the short-sighted experiment.

Speaking of indelible and burned, he also stared into the sun for interminable amounts of time, just to see what it would do. As story has it, he escaped that one unscathed as well.

RESISTANCE CHECKPOINT

Are you immersed in your work every day? Do you deliver the best of you? What you deliver will define you in the context of career—the results of your efforts will contribute to the options that can comprise a better way of life.

ALWAYS UNDER CONSTRUCTION

We can't sit on success. The methods, talents, and energies that contributed to our current station in life demanded discipline, habit, and risk. There are others who have discipline, habit, and are willing to risk and they will pursue what you have—that's how you got it, aggressive pursuit, and that's how you'll lose it, unless you keep moving forward.

"Success is always under construction." Companies will go under, relationships will change, and businesses will sell. Everything changes. It is part of the contract that is fine print for some and bold disclaimer for many, Always forward. If we are not moving forward, we will regress.

ACTION STEPS:

➜   Make something happen by knocking on doors and
    pressing flesh.

➜   Where possible, strive to get out and have a face-to-
    face conversation.

➜   Whether you serve internal or external clients, you
    need to engage with people. Too often we send
    internal emails to a person three doors down or avoid
    their calls or physical presence.

➜   Stretch, think, do—there is a power in its simplicity, a
    challenge in its execution, and a difference in its result.
    Walk down the hall, meet with your co-workers, have
    a discussion, not an email exchange.

A PHILOSOPHY FOR SUCCESS

The legend states that Jung, upon his split from Freud, returned
despondent to his childhood house and literally played in his
sandbox, the sandbox of his youth. The ability to recapture his
childlike wonder was, legend offers, one of the most salient
components in his ability to gain the clean, new perspective that
contributed to his development of archetypes and the founding of
analytical psychology.

Often, we get stuck on the treadmill of life. Play can
incite and rekindle the passion; it can rekindle and refuel our

spirit. It can summon our creative juices, relax our overworked brain circuitry, and spawn a new level of development.

We often experience a struggle in the search for passion and purpose. I think purpose and passion ensue from immersion into a process. There is a process from the worthy pursuit of what we do to achieve and create a better life for ourselves and our loved ones. Our business pursuits are but one component of our life—one which enables us to create lifestyle choices.

When we search and try to define passion and purpose, we confuse the concept for the feeling. The harder we search, the more elusive it becomes. The more we immerse ourselves in what we do, flowing with those elements that challenge us to create, collaborate with others and to flourish together, the closer we are drawn to the purpose and passion which define us. Passion and purpose are gifts to be enjoyed. They coalesce in the pursuit of a worthy endeavor. The endeavor can lead to the discovery. The discovery can occur when the pursuit is worthy and the process is undertaken with a spirit of obligation that is true to the self.

In my opinion, to follow the form of life in this manner is an antidote for the frustration and disappointment that comes from wanting, searching and believing that there is a prescribed universal formula; a sort of "one size fits all" that will direct us to these gifts. Beauty is found when we surrender to the pursuit.

Engaging with people who are passionate inspires the passion in those who hold this often elusive ineffable gift as precious. The discourse is often an indelible experience. Passion is found in the pursuit of that which embodies the quality of a person's life. The quality of life, in part, is about the pursuit of one's passions, the enjoyment of the process, and the ability to cherish the reward. If we are to live a life of meaning, we must limit our attempts to define the meaning of life and choose to live life.

To merely exist in a world of comfort and caution is like living by proxy. It is like assigning responsibility for your life to another person or surrendering to the whims and caprice of society at large. You will watch your life go by if you abrogate your right and obligation to live. If you are to live, live passionately. Invest and immerse yourself in the process of life. If you walk up to the pool and dip your toes in but never take the plunge, you will never learn to swim. Will you choose to dive in head first, immersed and invested? Learn how to swim.

We must extend the effort and attempt to share the knowledge with those who will give back and contribute. When we share the collage of experience and encourage the beginning or continuation of a quest for improvement, we can provide for the betterment of the whole.

You (and I) are here for a relatively short time. Live with no regrets. Engage with your foot pressing the proverbial pedal to the metal, with your tongue sensitive to the honeyed drops of rain. Listen with your ears deaf to dissension and your spirit untarnished by jealousy's disease. Know when to use your heart to hear, your mind to drive, and your visceral instincts to steer.

Capture each moment by allowing your eyes to become portals to your soul. Live life; savor it as the finest nectar. Overcome the fear and have the will to engage, summoning the wisdom to know when and with whom you choose to associate.

PART III

PLAY IT FORWARD

"The secret of change is to focus all of your energy, not on fighting the old, but on building the new."

— Socrates

MAINTAIN YOUR STRENGTH OF PURPOSE

Movies and books reveal the story of the hero's journey—overcoming adversity and triumphs to make a difference. Fear will keep us in the pit—but we need our fear because we can use our fear to motivate us to escape. There is a moving scene from The Dark Knight Rises, the final installment of Christopher Nolan's Batman trilogy starring Christian Bale. Bruce Wayne has been trapped in a prison at the bottom of a pit. The steep walls keep the prisoners at the bottom—they are allowed to attempt to climb out, though legend has it that only one—a child—has ever made it. After another failed attempt, a blind prisoner talks to Bruce about fear.

Batman is locked in mortal combat with his nemesis, Bane. During the one-sided struggle, Bane hoists Batman over his head, "I wondered what would break first, your spirit or your spine" he asks. With a resounding crack he drops the caped crusader over his knee. Bruce Wayne has his back broken, but Batman will not relinquish the fire of his spirit. The strength of purpose maintains the buoyancy of his spirit—it will serve him well in the pit. Bane consigns him to the squalor of a desolate prison. From the confines of the prison, Bruce Wayne begins to heal. The only way out of the pit, is through the top, where death is one slip or weakness of grip away.

One of the prisoners advises him that the way out of the pit to freedom is not about physical strength. "It is my body that makes the jump," replies Wayne. In the exchange the prisoner tells Wayne that fear is why he fails. He responds he is not afraid, he is angry.

The prisoner retorts, "Since you don't fear death you think this makes you strong, but how can you move faster and fight longer without the powerful impulse of the spirit, the fear of death?"

Bruce Wayne's fear is dying in the prison while Gotham City burns, with no one to save it. He must make the climb, find the fear and escape the pit. (Spoiler alert—Batman escapes the pit, using his fear as fuel to propel him forward.)

Before you can begin the ascent to success, you must escape from the pit of fear. I will not trick you into thinking it is easy. It's sticky and risky business —the more worthwhile the endeavor, the greater the obstacle to its realization. When things are obtained in an easy manner, I have found them to be lost in a similar manner. To face fear is to be bold—chance will favor the bold.

Life is to grow, step out of the shadows of the comfort zone, and into the light to face your fears again and again. Do the heavy lifting to defeat fear in private—in your internal pit. There is no safe position in life, there is just varying forms of struggle and alternate degrees of respite.

THE STUFF THAT HAPPENS BETWEEN THE SPACES

Words that fill the pages of books are just words—action is the stuff that happens between the spaces. In life, you can passively participate, observe from the sidelines, or actively engage to change the game.

Life is to have fun, and games are fun if you play them well. Sometimes people get too serious, which makes them play small; you need to put yourself out there, lighten up a little bit, and make it fun. Life is a game worth playing, learn to play it well.

Engagement is a participatory sport that demands we put ourselves in play, get in the game, face our fear, go forward, strive, and achieve. Before we can embrace the emotion of happiness, we must face the emotion of fear. How we respond and adapt to fear will strengthen our resolve in the present as it grows our resistance to it in the future. If we fear to risk, we lose the chance to obtain anything of worth. The victories are earned by those who engage in the game, run the risk of failure, and cash the emotional and physical checks from the reward of successful participation.

Remaining on the sidelines in life makes existence a spectator sport. It will be up to us to decide which risks are worth the rewards. For me, it would be fun to drive in a Formula One race, play quarterback for the Pittsburgh Steelers in an NFL game, or, racket in hand, be Centre Court at Wimbledon—but, for the record, I'd rather be a spectator at a bullfight.

WHEN FEAR IS NO LONGER A THREAT

Growth takes risk, and risk is accompanied by uncertainty and change. Uncertainty and loss are fear's elixir. We fear change and we attempt to avoid loss. But to grow is to lose the illusion of certainty and take a chance on change—success is earned outside of our comfort zone.

I am living to the spirit of the words that you read. As I begin a new adventure, one that is a marked departure from the business I started twenty-three years ago, I risk ego at a stage in my career where some are retiring on a remote beach. I think I have ego in perspective. I separate my self-image from the external and its unpredictable, uncontrollable vacillations and vicissitudes. There is something inside me that compels me to do what I love, and I am following my heart by living my purpose. The pages of this book are stamped in the ink of heart and framed by the design of purpose.

Life does not flourish in a vacuum. Step out of your circle and face your fear. Success is earned outside of your comfort zone. You will learn, if you haven't already, that you can't please everyone. Trying to please everyone is a recipe for frustration and failure. Give up the illusion that you can please everyone, honor yourself first, and respect your value system. Before you can earn the respect of others, establish, maintain, and remain anchored to your own self-respect. Self-respect can be diminished by desperation. Self-respect can be given away to those whom we believe have some magical power over us. There can be a referred power we assign to position, authority, or title. For some, those with celebrity status or deep pockets of material wealth seem to exist in a rarefied air. Understand that the magic is all in our minds—people are just people. We all end up the same way. Apply this and you will find new horizons, new friends, new mountains to climb—maintain your self-respect and go forward to create the best in life.

If you can confront and overcome your fears, you can create a better life, and generate more happiness, by facing and overcoming the dread that prevents its very existence. The quest for a better life moves through fear. Fear is the barrier we must move through to gain success and happiness in life. You and your fears are one. You can face and absorb their energy and move forward, or you can slink into the shadows and withdraw from life.

In my life, change and risk have always been a form of adrenaline and an elixir for achievement. When life can no longer threaten you with fear, you will be free to create, express, and make a difference for yourself by taking bold action.

MINDSET #2

I SHALL USE MY TIME

was walking through Sydney Harbor in Australia when a plaque embedded in the sidewalk stopped me cold in my tracks. It was a credo attributed to the American author, Jack London.

> *I would rather be ashes than dust!*
> *I would rather that my spark should burn out in a brilliant*
> *blaze than it should be stifled by dry-rot.*
> *I would rather be a superb meteor, every atom of me in*
> *magnificent glow, than a sleepy and permanent planet.*
> *The function of man is to live, not to exist.*
> *I shall not waste my days trying to prolong them.*
> *I shall use my time.*

After I read this quotation, I retreated to my favorite park bench in the harbor. I thought about the expanse of my career—the travail and the triumph, the challenge and the satisfaction of achievement. I thought about my journey out of the backwoods of Pennsylvania to the beaches of California. I thought about the fun I had in the fight and the strength I gained in the struggle to validate myself. Every year, I was determined to prove through achievement and the standings on the leader board that I belonged. A leader board can take the form of a newsletter or flier that some companies use to rank their sales force—it's a numbers game, a game where activity must create result because all that counts on the leader board is what you sold.

I began my career with $200 to my name, a suitcase, one corduroy suit, and two ties. For me, retreat wasn't an option; there was only one way—*Always Forward!* In two years, I "found a way and made a way" to become the top salesperson at Liberty Mutual—a company employing over 19,000 people at the time. I was ready for the "next challenge." I was recruited by and joined the sixth largest broker in the world, Corroon & Black (currently the Willis Group), where I fought every day to earn the coveted distinction as the top producer in the company. It was an award and designation I achieved for two consecutive years.

What a difference, a true departure, from the rough-hewn factory floor where I thought my future was foreclosed forever to the mahogany finish of Fortune 500 company board rooms. When I started in business, fresh out of graduate school, full of theory, but deficit in practice, I had two things to my name—a tremendous self-belief and an insatiable need to validate my self-worth through achievement.

I was loud and bold, a bit impudent perhaps, and I proclaimed to management in each firm with a prediction that I would be the top salesperson within two years. Separate companies, same prediction—a product of self-belief and a growing confidence from performance. I put myself out there, open to ridicule. People fear being ostracized and ridiculed and they fear the comfort of the known, opting for safety and security—they certainly don't want to call attention to themselves when the spotlight can reflect negatively. Fear can be a source of fuel, a compelling pull of purpose can move you through the greatest resistance. I would put fear in play with that proclamation—it became part of the fuel that drove me forward. I backed up my wild proclamation with results. In both cases, I reached my goal in the time predicted. The fear of being ridiculed trumped the resistance from rejection and propelled the activity that would rule success.

I'm the founder of a property and casualty insurance firm. We work with businesses whose revenues range from $10 million to over $1 billion. I've worked in the corporate insurance industry since college. I can state unequivocally, that many know more about the nuances of insurance coverage than I ever will. But I'll stand toe to toe with anyone on building relationships. Relationships are the essential element of a business—they are the rich tapestry that brings vibrancy to our life. I've pressed flesh in the corporate offices of American Express, Proctor and Gamble, Goodyear Tire, just to name a few. I can share with you that people in every company have fears. They get dressed the same way in the morning. They all have issues inside and outside of the office.

It doesn't matter what business you're in, someone has to create, sell, and service the product. People have to manage the process and deliver the product, generate the profit, and protect those margins every day—we're all in sales. No payroll is met unless something is first sold. Each day, in every facet of our life we convince, sell, and enroll people to our point of view. We negotiate and live in a world of compromise solutions. Where are we going to dinner? What movie do you want to see? Who's taking the kids to school today? Who has the kids this weekend? Who can help me? Who can I help? Why should I help? Why would you help? How can I help? Everything involves selling. You don't get something in life without giving something up. It's the rule of trade-off. We sell ourselves every day, from the way we dress, to what we say, what we do, and how we do it.

This book is the product of the lessons I learned from the green, optimistic rookie of the past to the realistic veteran in the present. From the time I stepped forth into the world of business, I started doing things, taking mental notes, making mistakes, learning, making more mistakes, and applying the lessons of the experience. It was an expensive lesson, more so emotionally than financially. I failed early and I failed often. As a matter of fact, I failed on my first thirteen sales attempts. Each time I failed I was learning. What I learned is how to win. My optimism never waned. My willingness to learn from defeat expanded with each failed attempt. What I've learned I am sharing in this book as I have in my company for over twenty-three years. I want to share so others can prosper and grow. I don't want the lessons to die inside of me. I don't want the music to die with me.

Sitting on that park bench, I thought about the limited universe that I coached, mentored, and led. I felt this deep need

to share this lesson, and I committed to doing whatever it took
to make this happen. Today, I hop on planes and I give talks
across the United States. Tomorrow, these talks will be conducted
internationally. You may think, "Well, okay, this stuff worked for
you, but how do you know if it will make a difference for me?"
I know it will work for you if you understand the extent of the
sacrifice you must make to succeed. No matter what business
you're in, you cannot sustain forward movement without the
continual commitment to give and do the best you can every
day—no retreat, no surrender. If you can live to the spirit of
this commitment, you will experience a significant difference in
both your business and personal pursuits from the philosophies,
processes, strategies and methods that are outlined in detail in
Always Forward.

I think money and happiness are often mutually
exclusive. Money can bring short-term joy, but lasting happiness
comes from the inside. It's how we view the world, what we take
in, what we make of it, how resilient we are, and how realistic
we make our expectations. Money can enable the conditions
for happiness by eliminating or limiting the impediments that
prevent its very existence. But money cannot give happiness. I
think when we eliminate the obstacles to happiness, the financial
frustration and day-to-day stress of debt load, we lessen our
anxiety, and release ourselves from a servile disposition based
solely upon survival. Happiness is a condition that we create by
eliminating those things which hinder our personal expression
and precludes the enjoyment of life. People seek happiness but

I think it is found and experienced when we don't search, when we are open to express ourselves free of stress and worry, free to share, unencumbered by the heavy weight of personal burden.

From that park bench, I thought about what was most important to me. What's most important is to share these lessons, these secrets so you can make better choices from a bigger pool of options. They say that people who go to the grave and don't share what they've learned take everything with them. The people who share what they've learned leave something behind. This is the true essence of legacy—leave the lessons and experience behind for others to benefit and prosper from. Choose to make the world a better place than you found it.

The lion's instinct is to be free. Our instinct is to fear. Fear attempts to hold us captive. We may never be free of its specter, but we can alter our future by overcoming its thrall in the present. Fear likes to remind us of the outcomes and people who fell short of our goal and disappointed us. It points to the past to provide the murky unrest of resistance in the present. It is easy to corroborate what we choose not to do today with a disappointment in our past.

People stay in jobs they can't stand and relationships they endure. They exist; they don't live. They fear change, resist the unknown, and resign to the discomfort of the familiar. Life goes out of them just as it did for the lion in that zoo—the flame of vitality soon turns into the flicker of despair. The flame is the spirit, the soul, the life force.

I am not advocating a rebellion against nature; rather, I am encouraging an alignment with it. For some, the comfort of familiarity is a place to flourish, where vibrancy of purpose exists. For others, comfort is accompanied by an instinctual pull, a gnawing tug that may be ignored or discounted by the distractions that disguise themselves as short-term, illusory happiness. True happiness ensues when our external representation is in alignment with our core identity. Every impulse, everything we think and do, either maintains, brings us closer, or moves us further from who we are at our very core.

Writers fear leaving the better book in their heads. Will your best possible life fill the pages of the book you author every day? The time is now to express, create, and change your life. When you change your life by continuing to evolve, you will change the lives of others. Do the work. Hone your resilience, strengthen your willpower and cultivate the persistence necessary to prevail. In the dark recesses of thought, fears will seep through the crevices of memory and extend themselves as the tendrils of future limitations. It will be darkest before the light, but when we face our fears, what will come forth is the courage, awareness, and resolve to absorb their energy and move forward to create the best possible life. Don't fear to begin, but rather fear the future regret of failing to embark.

Until we meet again, face your fears and go "Always Forward!"

ACKNOWLEDGMENTS

With extreme gratitude for the collaborative efforts of Addy Hanson, without her nimble fingers, discerning eye, and constructive feedback, I would still be contemplating a book from the fringes of possibility. Her indefatigable work ethic made progress possible, as she brought stability to circles of swirling thought, clarity to the obscure narrative, and a calm that balanced the frustration of creative delay.

To my editor and friend, Henry DeVries—a book about fear was your idea. Thank you, by the way, for the pain—the gain was worth it. I learned enough about fear, the mind, and the brain to think about becoming a neuroscientist. Only IQ would hold me back, not will. It's difficult to contain lightning, but you found a big enough bottle. Thank you for keeping me focused, on point, and moving forward.

To our clients—without you, people like me couldn't write books like this. You are what make our business existence possible.

To all of my fellow co-workers at The Wooditch Group, thank you for making the enterprise better by rendering me redundant.

ABOUT THE AUTHOR

Bill Wooditch is a mentor and advocate for those who actively seek and are determined to make a difference in their lives and the lives of others. He earned his bachelor's degree in psychology at Purdue University and his master's degree in public administration at Penn State.

He began his career on the phones, knocking on doors, and pressing flesh as he "found a way and made a way" to become the top salesperson for two companies—Liberty Mutual and Corroon & Black Insurance Services (currently the Willis Group). He started his privately owned firm in 1993, a company that he continues to lead today through active recruiting, training, and mentoring.

He is the founder, CEO, and president of The Wooditch Group, a privately held risk management and insurance services firm. The Wooditch Group provides client-centric solutions and comprehensive risk management programs for domestic and international clients whose revenues range from $10 million to over $3 billion.

He is also the founder of Think Next, Act Now!, a learning forum that trains tomorrow's entrepreneurs today. Think Next, Act Now! develops the strategy and teaches the techniques to inspire and motivate personal and corporate growth. His engaged leadership continues to enroll and enable people to achieve their dreams by continually challenging them to find their why, define the what, and execute the how to achieve.

He specializes in the development, coaching, and mentorship of sales professionals and leaders in business. He is personally active in the recruitment, training, and mentoring of today's determined advocates and tomorrow's entrepreneurs and leaders. He has developed a proprietary system that is proven, continually tested, and refined against the ultimate system of measurement that is termed the "bottom line."

He is a dynamic, high-energy speaker. His keynote speeches and training sessions are designed and dedicated to deliver the means and methods to achieve peak-performance in business and life pursuits. To date, his talks have included, but are not limited to, leadership, sales, teamwork, and customer service. He delivers knowledge with intention and purpose of conviction.

To inquire about bulk book discounts or booking Bill Wooditch as a speaker, please email alwaysforward@wooditch. com or call 949.553.9800.

Made in the USA
Charleston, SC
28 April 2016